ADVANCE PRAISE

"Finally! An expert in digital marketing who is on my side!"

—KEITH J. CUNNINGHAM, AUTHOR
OF THE ROAD LESS STUPID

"Innovate or your business dies. The capitalist world is sorting out winners and losers faster than ever. Phillip does a great job singling out strategies that have proven effective for some of the best in business, and distilled them into an easy-to-capture format."

—PETER MALLOUK, PRESIDENT OF CREATIVE
PLANNING AND NAMED ONE OF WORTH MAGAZINE'S
"TOP 100 MEN AND WOMEN IN GLOBAL FINANCE"

"With so much information and noise coming at us every second of the day, it's terrific to have a book that gives us a workable, practical approach for grasping the insights to guide us to success. Fire Them Now: 7 Secrets Digital Marketers Sell not only provides the formula for winning; it also is filled with real-world examples to illustrate it. If you're going to win in today's hyper-tough political and business environment, you better outthink your competitors, and Phillip Stutts shows you how. It's the winning approach."

—PETER KLEIN, AUTHOR OF THINK TO WIN

"I've been a Phillip Stutts fan for years. He's one of the very few people who understands deeply the marketing and public relations worlds of both politics and of business. As such, he has much to teach those of us who play in only one of those worlds. In Fire Them Now he shares some of his best ideas in a fast-paced and engaging style."

—DAVID MEERMAN SCOTT, MARKETING STRATEGIST AND BEST-SELLING AUTHOR OF THE NEW RULES OF MARKETING AND PR

"Pray your marketing agency reads this before you do, or they should be fired."

—JAY ABRAHAM, FOUNDER AND CEO OF ABRAHAM GROUP INC.

"There is no one who knows more about digital marketing agencies and what they do wrong than Phillip Stutts. If you spend money with a digital marketing agency, you need to drop everything and read this book right now."

—TUCKER MAX, #1 NEW YORK TIMES BEST-SELLING AUTHOR AND COFOUNDER OF BOOK IN A BOX

"I'm from the other side of the political aisle, but I can tell you without reservation that the advice in Fire Them Now transcends partisanship. Phillip Stutts uncovers the truth about how to truly win big in business with unflinching honesty and humor. Best of all, it's not just empty platitudes. He provides *you with actual tools to succeed. Fire Them Now is essential reading for anyone in business or politics."*

—DONNA BRAZILE, POLITICAL STRATEGIST, AL GORE 2000 CAMPAIGN MANAGER, FORMER CHAIRWOMAN OF THE DEMOCRATIC NATIONAL COMMITTEE, AND AUTHOR OF HACKS: THE INSIDE STORY OF THE BREAK-INS AND BREAKDOWNS THAT PUT DONALD TRUMP IN THE WHITE HOUSE

"Phillip Stutts is a regular guest on my ESPN TV and radio show, and I find him smart, funny, and totally entertaining. Fire Them Now is an incredibly insightful look at how political strategies can transform digital media marketing. It's a must-read!"

—PAUL FINEBAUM, HOST ON ESPN AND BEST-SELLING AUTHOR OF MY CONFERENCE CAN BEAT YOUR CONFERENCE: WHY THE SEC STILL RULES COLLEGE FOOTBALL

"Hard-hitting and to the point, Fire Them Now will become the gold standard for negotiating with marketing and PR firms and setting the metrics for performance-based success for your business. Phillip Stutts's book is the new disruptor in how to prepare for change and excel in the new business model that will define survival in the twenty-first-century marketplace."

—CDR KIRK S. LIPPOLD, USN (RET.), AUTHOR OF FRONT BURNER: AL QAEDA'S ATTACK ON THE USS COLE

FIRE THEM NOW

FIRE
THEM NOW

THE 7 LIES DIGITAL MARKETERS SELL...AND THE TRUTH ABOUT POLITICAL STRATEGIES THAT HELP BUSINESSES WIN

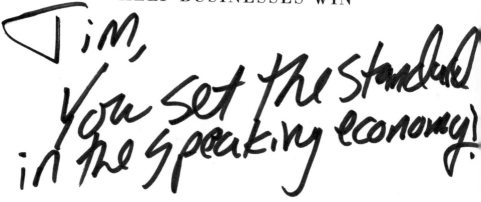

Jim,
You set the standard
in the speaking economy!

PHILLIP STUTTS

LIONCREST

PUBLISHING

FIRE THEM NOW

The 7 Lies Digital Marketers Sell...And the Truth about
Political Strategies that Help Businesses Win

ISBN   978-1-61961-887-9 *Hardcover*

978-1-61961-886-2 *Paperback*

978-1-61961-885-5 *Ebook*

To Parker—two people were born when you arrived. I love you.

CONTENTS

ACKNOWLEDGMENTS

First, I want to acknowledge my wife, Annie. Not sure where I'd be without you, and I'm grateful for your support and the journey we're on. Thank you. I love you.

I want to thank two people I've never met but to whom I owe a lifetime of gratitude: Tim Ferriss and Tony Robbins. After reading *The 4-Hour Workweek*, I decided to define life on my terms. It was the start of an epic journey. Thank you, Tim. In the fall of 2014, I started listening to a podcast interview with Tony Robbins, and within ten minutes, I had pulled my car over and was taking notes. An hour later, I was on the phone with Tony Robbins's office figuring out how to go to new heights. It has led me to passionately pursue growth, love, and contribution. Life forever changed for me that day. Thank you, Tony.

Jay Abraham, Peter Diamandis, David Meerman Scott, Chad Cooper, and Keith Cunningham all define preeminence in business and loyal friendship. Thank you.

I also want to thank Tucker Max, who was beyond kind, helpful, and generous in leading me through the book process. His honesty and loyalty are traits that would make this world a better place if we all practiced them.

To the amazing Book in a Box team—Zach Obront, JT McCormick, John Vercher, Meghan McCracken, and Mark Chait—I'm so very grateful.

Thanks to my badass team at Go BIG Media and Win BIG Media—Dean Petrone, Brent Barksdale, Daniel Bassali, Nicole Venezia, Andrew Gordon, Peter Graves, Ashley Harvey, Kurt Pickhardt, Jess Wilson, Becca Conti, JD King, Elliot Fuchs, Nicole Fryling, Jill Greenwald, Jared Soloman, and everyone else on my team that pitched in. These amazing souls are building the best culture of any business in the country. There is no other team out there with whom I'd rather grow and serve.

Many thanks to those who were interviewed for the book and provided amazing insight, including Pete Hegseth, Donna Brazile, David Meerman Scott, Peter Klein, Peter Mallouk, and Keith Cunningham.

My gratitude to those who inspire me on a daily basis is beyond words. These purpose-driven souls include: James Altucher, Lewis Howes, Dave Asprey, Tom Bilyeu, Paul Finebaum, Joe Polish, Peter Diamandis, Dan Sullivan, Lance Armstrong, Noah Kagan, Ryan Daniel Moran, Gary Vaynerchuk, Neil Strauss, Reid Hoffman, Guy Raz, Jay Mohr, Adam Carolla, Drew Pinskey, Joe Rogan, Clay Travis, Seth Godin, Ed Hallowell, Ryan Holiday, Oren Klaff, Auren Hoffman, Marc Andreessen, Steven Gundry, Marshall Goldsmith, Rosamund and Benjamin Zander, Geoff Smart, Randy Street, Keith Rabois, Matt Lewis, Marcus Lemonis, Mark Cuban, Nick Saban, Arianna Huffington, and Peter Thiel.

And thanks to those with whom I've worked in the past who shaped me today: George W. Bush, Bobby and Supriya Jindal, John Thune, Richard Shelby, George W. Bush, Dan Quayle, Curt and Wes Anderson, Brad Todd, Rolfe McCollister Jr., Rob Collins, Chip Saltsman, Doug McGinn, Matt Well, Taylor Gross, Michael Golden, Ward Baker, Jean Skaane, Rod Paige, Brian Jones, Matt Zabel, Gene Hickok, Richard Norman, Larry Russell, Ken Mehlman, Blaise Hazelwood, Betsy DeVos, Greg Brock, John Schilling, Carlos Lopez-Cantera, Senator Richard Shelby, Kirk Lippold, Chad Mathis, Garret Graves, Steve Scalise, Karl Rove, Lauren Perry, Kelli Bottger, Tom Young, Ray Cole, Brian Jodice, Jessica Bohn, Chris Carr, John Truchard,

Oscar Renteria, Erin DeLullo, Gary Coby, John Bailey, Brian Jones, John Kirtley, Kevin Chavous, Lindsey Rust, Matt Frendewey, Michael Allen, Shane D'Aprile, Stewart Hall, Zack Dawes, John Danielson, Kyle McSlarrow, Todd Lamb, Alex Vogel, Julian Flannery, Brian Nick, Andrew Kaplan, Jack Oliver, Mike Duffey, and Rich Beeson.

Finally, thanks to all the other family and friends who helped me along the way, especially Britton Stutts, Evelyn Stutts, Gene Stutts, Paul Belair, Cody Foster, Stewart Webb, Andy Puckett, Trey Echols, Lola Bryce, Jamey Price, Reynolds Henderson, John Giles, Vince Conrad, Maxx Bricklin, Anne Marie Malecha, Steve Walsh, Kav Tucker, Steve Twohig, Alex Klein, Bill Carmody, Dan Levy, Jim Holbrook, John Hayes, Jonathan Nikkila, Judd Jackson, Marcus Shingles, Matt Mackowiak, Sandi Cunningham, Tony Breitbach, Danny Markstein, Rob and Ati Williams, Christopher Hogin, Adriel Domenech, Paul Barkett, Eric Peters, Steve Forsythe, Reverend Louis Leon, Albert Finch, Brad Hester, Conan French, Matt Hunter, and Michael Gee.

FOREWORD

BY JAY ABRAHAM

I have devoted my entire professional career to the discovery and sharing of higher, better, safer, and far more success-certain ways to grow a business.

I've studied 500+ industries looking for universal principles my clients could either add or replace to whatever market, strategy, and/or promotional approaches they currently use.

That gave way to legendary concepts like *3 Ways to Grow a Business*, *The Power Parthenon of Exponential Growth*, *The Sticking Point Solution*, and *Power Principles*.

That said, I've examined and evaluated the methodology

Phillip Stutts has developed to win highly competitive—win, or lose, only—political campaigns. Phillip's approach wins almost every election.

If it can do that in a mere matter of months for a political candidate, I'm convinced it can be epic if used properly by any profit-oriented enterprise and entrepreneur. Phillip and his methodologies are the real thing.

JAY ABRAHAM

As Founder and CEO of Abraham Group, Inc., Jay Abraham has helped grow more than four hundred companies, including IBM, Microsoft, Citibank, and Charles Schwab, and has significantly increased the bottom lines of over 10,000 clients in more than 7,000 industries worldwide.

INTRODUCTION

In 2012, I was diagnosed with a rare esophageal disease called Achalasia. It affects one out of 100,000 people, and skews toward an older population, so the odds of me having it were even crazier when you consider that I was thirty-eight years old at the time.

What's Achalasia, you ask? Basically, the nerves in my esophagus are dead, and so the muscles don't contract to push food down into my stomach. Anything I eat gets stuck. The only way to get food down is to drink tons of liquid. I tell people that my esophagus looks like an upside-down cheerleader's pom-pom; it's curved into a J shape, and totally shredded at the bottom.

There is no cure.

When I was diagnosed, it was a huge shock to my system. More than shocking, it was frustrating, because my doctors couldn't seem to identify the root cause of the disease. My initial response was one of paralysis. I was filled with fear and uncertainty about what this disease meant for my future, and for my family's future; I was bitter with resentment that, even though I've always been meticulous about my health, I'd somehow been afflicted with such a rare and debilitating autoimmune condition at such a young age.

So, what did I do? I stuck my head in the sand, and essentially handed over the keys to my disease.

I didn't do any outside research; I didn't seek a second or third opinion. I turned over management of my disease to other people and let them do the heavy lifting. I took all the pills my doctors prescribed without question, or really without any deeper understanding of what pills I was taking and why. I took a massive daily dose of antacids while continuing to eat all the foods I'd always eaten, and that had been tearing up my gut and making my esophageal problem worse.

I hate taking medicine. I understand that, in many cases, it's absolutely crucial, but for me, it feels like a Band-Aid rather than a roadmap. When you take a pill, for every benefit you get out of it, there's a tradeoff. With the anti-heartburn medicine I was shoveling down my throat by the truckload, there is evidence of long-term links to dementia—basically, the theory is that when you kill all the bad "acid" in your body, you also kill off the good kind that feeds your brain. By mindlessly handing over control to my doctors and allowing them to Band-Aid the problem rather than discover the source and make a plan, I was digging myself deeper into prolonged suffering.

As encouraged by my doctors, I had three major surgeries (and fifteen additional minor procedures). The first two major surgeries failed. That's right—failed. My doctors told me that I was the first person they'd seen fail two esophageal surgeries, and I told them that, after all, coming in first was my business.

I was told that a fourth surgery would be "dicey." I began eating two meals a day entirely in liquid form, and supplementing with an ever-present handful of antacids.

In August 2016, I headed to the Mayo Clinic for a one-year checkup on the third surgery I'd had, called a Heller Myotomy with Fundoplication (say that five times fast!). It had been an invasive surgery, to say the least—even today, the outside of my stomach looks like I've been in a knife fight, with five incision scars fighting for space.

This third surgery in 2015 at Mayo had had to be done because my useless esophagus had actually curved like a banana. Food was not emptying into my stomach and, in addition to the discomfort, it was fermenting and eroding my esophagus. According to my doctors, they had to straighten it out, or I was on a slippery slope to esophageal cancer. Thus, I elected to have my third major surgery in twenty-six months.

Have you ever recovered from a major surgery? Going under the knife again wasn't a decision I made lightly. The dread was palpable, but I had no choice. I just wanted to get it over with and thrive again.

A year later, at the checkup, I was told that the work they'd done on my esophagus looked stable, but that it *would* come undone one day, and that without a cure, a feeding tube was something I should plan for.

A feeding tube? *Are you kidding me?*

It was in that moment, sitting in the Mayo Clinic offices, that I had an epiphany. I decided right then and there that I was done being a bystander to my disease. I just couldn't accept that a cure was impossible, and that all I could do was just wait around for a feeding tube, all the while taking massive doses of a medicine that might ultimately give me dementia.

What the fuck are you doing? I asked myself.

I made a decision: I had to figure out this disease. I had to take control of it. I wasn't going to let it take control of me anymore.

In late January of 2017, I attended Peter Diamandis's Abundance 360 summit. He holds this three-day summit each year for his Abundance 360 community of entrepreneurs and investors. These are committed executives who want to learn more about upcoming disruptive technologies, and how to take advantage of the very shifts in the global economy that terrify most business owners I meet.

Peter introduced the concept of the "moonshot." In popular terminology, a moonshot is a hugely ambitious, groundbreaking project launched without any expectation of profit, or even success, in the short term. Sitting in the audience that day, listening to Peter passionately describe his moonshots, I realized that I had one of my own.

I was going to cure my uncurable disease.

Sure, I had no idea where to start. Sure, all my doctors had shrugged, told me variations of "it is what it is," and shoved prescription-strength medications into my hands. But, if anything, the seeming hopelessness of the situation was what fueled me. This was a huge, crazy, impossible goal, and I was going to throw everything I had at it.

I worked on the concept of my moonshot for weeks after I returned from the summit. I collected reams of research and talked to experts, and decided to write a digital article about my experience. After all, when I'd been diagnosed, there hadn't been much out there by way of discussion when I went looking. The article was placed in *Inc. Magazine* about a month later. As part of the placement—the digital marketer in me unable to resist—we targeted audiences we thought might contain people who could lend some insight, or help work toward my moonshot of finding a cure. We put together a small digital advertising budget, and we targeted Silicon Valley, Los Angeles, and Washington, D.C.

A few weeks later, a woman who headed up an international Achalasia Awareness organization based in Los Angeles emailed me saying that she had read my article, and asked for a phone call.

On the phone, she said, "So, you know there's no cure for this, right? There's never been a cure."

"Yeah, yeah, yeah," I told her. "I know that."

She paused. Then she said, "Okay. But you plan to cure it?"

"Yes," I said.

"And how do plan to do that?"

"Right now, I have no idea. But I've been reading a lot about stem cells, and I think that could be worth a shot."

I couldn't tell whether she was impressed by the research I'd done, or humoring my delusional thinking; but she said, "Tell you what. I know Achalasia doctors all over the country. I'll call around, and see what some of them think about stem cells."

A week later, she called me back. "Guess what?"

It turned out that a doctor she knew at Johns Hopkins, who'd been working on Achalasia research for twenty years, had told her he thought stem cells were going to be the cure.

She introduced me to him. One thing led to another, and a few months later, I found myself the subject of a proposed one-man clinical trial, having my esophagus injected with stem cells on a regular basis in an attempt to regenerate the muscles and nerves.

I had started with one small step, and it had become one

giant leap toward achieving my moonshot. And it had started with *innovation*. I'd been told "this is the way it is," by the best esophageal doctors in the world—and I'd tried something else. I'd taken control of my own fate instead of waiting for the tidal wave to crash over my head.

WORKING FOR THE WIN

When I was diagnosed with my disease, I stuck my head in the sand and tried to ignore the problem. The funny thing is, this is *exactly* the opposite of how I've operated in my career, and if ignoring problems *had* been my habit, there's no way I would ever have found success.

I've spent over twenty years working as a marketing strategist and consultant in the world of professional politics. Put simply, I get candidates elected.

Let's get one thing out of the way right up front: while I've worked with clients from both sides of the aisle, I primarily come from the world of *Republican* politics. And I'm proud of it. I've seen enormous successes, painful failures, and immense strength of character and leadership in the more than twenty years of my career so far.

However, I know that we're living in a particularly volatile political climate, so I want to state right up front that this book *isn't* about partisanship. The ideas, strategies, and tactics in this book have no party affiliation at all—both Republicans and Democrats use these strategies, because it's how you win. In fact, throughout this book, the research and interviews I conducted represent both sides of the aisle.

When a client comes calling, they don't want to contract my services because of my party affiliation. They want to hire me because they know I'll do everything in my power to get them the outcome they're looking for.

These strategies *work,* no matter what your politics are. More importantly, these strategies can transform your business.

On its face, politics is really no different from business. The candidate is the product; the campaign platform is the mission statement. The voter is the customer. In both politics and business, you need to tell a story that resonates with your audience. The only difference between politics and business is that, if anything, it's *more difficult* to reach the customer in the political world—and as such, successful political marketers are really extraordinarily good at it.

If a customer is persuaded to buy a new brand of soda, or

switch to a different brand of computer, and they wind up not liking their choice, they have options. They can get their money back, or simply stop using the product. In politics, there's no getting your money back—or at the very least, not for a couple of years. Voters are stuck with their choice for anywhere from two to six years, and as such, they prize that choice above all. Being able to influence people on the political level is the Mecca of branding, influence, and conversion.

And yet, for years, corporate digital marketers have been perceived as the Goliath of practitioners. This perception is spurred on by their multimillion-dollar clients locked into years-long contracts and the modern, hip workplaces that give the impression of being ahead of the times. Meanwhile, the political marketing world is seen as David, the scrappy underdog, with short-term, come-and-go campaigns, and constant volatility in the marketplace (and let's face it, Brooks Brothers and penny loafers aren't exactly the fashion of the now—but hey, we don't have time to think about the latest clothing trends!).

This narrative is outdated, but it's exactly the perception your business digital marketing firm wants you to have. They don't want the narrative to change because it works in their favor, and allows them to do the minimum work for maximum revenue.

The foundation of political digital marketing is to be nimble, adaptable, proactive, and outcome-based. In politics, we have one goal, and one goal only: *we have to win.*

If we don't win, we won't get hired again. Who wants to hire a marketer who loses?

The only way we can stay ahead of the game and bring home that win is to constantly innovate, test, refine, and find the most precise and effective ways of persuading the voters. Speed is everything—we're working on a timeline unlike anything in the business world. Our goal isn't some vaguely defined "future success;" it's a deadline with pinpoint accuracy: Election Day.

With a looming Election Day every two years, political digital marketing experts have a scorecard. They are held accountable on a cyclical and incredibly short timeline. If you lose too many times, you're out of business—put simply, you win, or you die.

If you're a business owner, run a non-profit, or lead the marketing team for a company, wouldn't you want to work with a team that employs this kind of marketing attitude?

The very nature of our business has created a mindset that political marketers live and breathe with every action they take. They are entirely outcome-focused, and put every ounce of energy they have into executing for their client. They work for the win, no matter what it takes, because their candidate's win is *their* win. And it's laid bare for the world to see. Our record is public record. When we win, everyone in our industry knows it. When we lose, everyone in our industry knows it. That's accountability at the highest level.

Again, this is why it doesn't matter what side of the aisle you're on—if you can win campaigns, you're in demand. One apprehensive friend recently asked me if being a Republican or Democrat would prevent certain companies or businesses from working with political marketers.

My response? *No way!*

The companies who work with political marketers are in the game to win, not to align with an ideology. And with this book, my aim is to help you, not divide your thinking. But if my party affiliation is still too much for you to bear, I understand. Put this book down. Continue with the current marketing strategy that every other business employs. Don't be an outlier.

Your competition will learn the smartest strategies on the

planet while you, like so many other entrepreneurs, stick your head in the sand.

I understand the instinct to avoid what scares you and stick your head in the sand—but it's not going to get you where you want to go.

SHIFT HAPPENS

Right now, when it comes to the global economy, the vast majority of businesses are fighting uphill, and most of them don't know it or want to ignore it. Many think they're sitting pretty up top. But new technology, like AI, robots, and the massive transformative disruptions of the digital age have placed most existing businesses at such a disadvantage that there is now an unseen expiration date on their business model. Countless businesses that have been mainstays for the past twenty to fifty years won't even exist in the next decade. Many jobs that people rely on today won't exist in five years.

No business, no industry, will be spared this disruption, and the only option is to plan for it and adapt. You can see it as an opportunity—but *only* if you take action now.

Innovation is not just a "should" but a "must" if you want

your business not just to survive the coming changes, but to thrive in the new economy.

Radical shifts in the economy are happening at this very moment, and there's nothing you can do to stop them. It's more important than ever to innovate in the face of change—but how do you go about doing that?

Digital marketing firms know that you're confused, and they count on you being nervous enough to sign on for whatever solution they provide. But are those solutions really aimed at helping your business, not just survive the coming tidal wave of disruption, but surf it all the way in to a win?

If you're being told by your digital marketing firm that you *have* to rely on their services to survive, not only are you being deceived, but you're putting all your hope and trust in one direction—the wrong one.

The shift in my professional life from politics to business was almost an accident, but looking back, it was also inevitable.

Here's a great example of what I'm talking about—and coincidentally, this story was also the tipping point for me in moving from strictly political marketing into the world of marketing for businesses.

But first, let me ask you a business question: if you were trying to sell houses in Hawaii, the first place you'd put an ad is the *Wall Street Journal's* print edition, right?

If you're confused, believe me—so was I, when I heard this client's story.

A few years ago, my digital marketing firm began a relationship with a real estate development company in Hawaii. They'd just begun a huge project, building an entire new residential neighborhood along the coast of two of the state's islands and wanted to build buzz among the kinds of people who would buy a home on the beach in Hawaii.

Before they came to us, they were advised by their marketing team to cut a five-figure check in order to purchase a single ad in the real estate section of the *Wall Street Journal*.

Not knowing any better—and why should they? Expertise is why they have a marketing team in place!—the client was, at first, thrilled. *We're going to be in the Wall Street Journal! How cool is that? What a huge win!*

Think about it for a second: who reads the *Wall Street Journal* print edition? Primarily people on the east coast.

The five-figure ad buy netted this Hawaii real estate

development company precisely one new lead, which subsequently didn't convert. It was a total flop.

The client's marketing team came back to them and said, "Now that we know that advertising Hawaii real estate to East Coast markets doesn't work, we want to do some more testing to see what *will* work. We'll need another big investment to really do a thorough job, enter into the digital space, and figure out what's going to bring you the sales you want."

The client was frustrated, confused, and most of all, bitter; they knew deep down that their money was being thrown right down the drain. They'd spent their budget on an ego play, and they had nothing to show for it. But they were torn—*these guys are the experts, right? What's the alternative to doing whatever they say?*

Luckily, one of the partners had been exposed to the world of political marketing, and had the spark of an idea. He reached out to me and said, "I'm fascinated by what you guys do in politics. My marketing team is getting me nowhere—is there maybe a way you can apply your political strategies to my business, and help me get a better ROI?"

(The answer, by the way, was *yes*—but you'll need to keep

reading to hear exactly how political strategies transformed his business!)

Until that point, I'd only ever worked on marketing political candidates, but I'd always suspected that the techniques I used in politics could work just as well for companies. The trouble was, businesses, in my experience, were incredibly afraid of change, and were absolutely paralyzed by that fear. Nobody wanted to think different and try something new.

These days, that's changed. With the rapidly shifting economy and the major disruptions coming down the line for nearly every single industry, businesses are open to new ideas. They're less afraid of standing out, and more interested in winning.

THE PARALYSIS OF FEAR

Fear leads to bad decisions. A decision made out of fear is *never* going to be a good decision in the long run.

(Okay, sometimes a fear-based decision is the right one, I'll admit. By all means, allow your fear to send you running out of a burning building.)

Here's why many digital marketers are selling you a bill of

goods: *because they know they can.* They're in it for their paycheck, not for your business. They have little motivation to ensure your success—their only goal is to fulfill the terms of their contract, and if they can do that by dazzling you with flashy creative and an advertising campaign that strokes your ego, even if it produces precisely *zero* leads, they will.

Put simply, most digital marketing firms are taking advantage of their clients, day in and day out, with every hour they bill. They're working for *their* needs first, and yours second. How many hours does it really take to come up with a winning media strategy? How many meetings could possibly be required to brainstorm and collaborate on that strategy? How long does it take to write it up and pass it around for edits before presenting it to the client? I'll give you a hint: take whatever number of hours your digital firm has charged you for such work, reduce it to a fifth of that number, and you're closer to the truth. The truth doesn't matter, though—you still got charged five times more than the work required!

The vast majority of digital marketing firms overcharge, under deliver, and work for their own needs rather than the needs of their clients. When I crossed over into the business world from the world of politics, the amount of sheer waste and lies I saw in the practices of competing digital marketing firms blew my mind.

Not just that: it *pissed me off.*

That anger is what led me to write this book. Watching clients and friends get, frankly, ripped off by digital marketing firms who preyed on their fear of economic disruption, or their ignorance to technology advances in the digital marketplace that they couldn't keep up with—and then delivered zero ROI—made me furious. Over the course of the last three years, I've interviewed and discussed this topic with more than one hundred CEOs from various levels of business, from small shops to Fortune 500 companies. They've all told me about the same experiences with digital marketing firms. They describe being frustrated, lost, feeling like they've been taken advantage of, and fearful of the coming industry disruption for which they're not as prepared as they'd like to be.

If this sounds familiar to you, or you're nodding your head in solidarity, then reading this book might be the most important thing you do for your business this year.

WHY THIS BOOK?

I've spent my life working on and carefully studying enormously successful campaigns. All of them share universal truths, certain strategies that translate to a win no matter how people implement them. I wrote this book to show you these strategies, and open your eyes to the ways you've been misled by the status quo of the digital marketing industry establishment.

The very characteristics and constraints that make political marketing seem like David to business marketing's Goliath—fast-cycling campaigns, constant churn—are exactly the elements that put political marketing on the path that outpaces corporate digital marketing. Political marketers lead the way in innovation and ROI, and not only that, they're *way ahead* of the business world.

The two most important factors you need to focus on to explode your business are obvious: innovation and marketing. That's why this book is for entrepreneurs, small business owners, non-profit leaders and marketers.

There are no greater experts on innovation and marketing than political marketers. In this book, I take the universal truths about how we win and apply them to business. I also highlight successful CEOs and businesses that operate with a political mindset to prove that it works. The lessons you'll learn in this book will help you to adapt to the coming disruption, save your business, and most importantly, make it thrive.

Here's what this book is: a way for committed business

owners to look behind the curtain of political marketing and see how the success-driven strategies of political marketers are the key to explosive business growth. It's a push to take your head out of the sand, innovate, and shine a light on what your digital marketing team is doing—or *not* doing—for your business.

Here's what this book *isn't*: A get-rich-quick scheme, a guide to playing the algorithm game, or a manual of specific social media platform tactics to use that might be obsolete in six months.

To win, you don't need to know the digital ad space inside and out. You simply need to shift your understanding and focus—let go of your paralysis and take action to get into the game.

I've been where you are. I was dealt a huge blow when I was diagnosed with my disease, and my reaction to fear was to stick my head in the sand and pretend it wasn't happening. I know all too well the frustration, anxiety, and confusion that comes from being faced with a problem you don't know how to solve. But through my political marketing career, I've also seen the solution, and I know that taking back control of your outcome and shifting your mindset toward innovation are the crucial first steps on the path to success.

THE 7 LIES DIGITAL MARKETERS TELL YOU—AND HOW POLITICAL STRATEGIES ARE THE SOLUTION

Most marketing firms have an agenda to put their needs and payday ahead of your outcome. This leads to poor decision-making, mismanaged marketing, and deception. They're lying to you—but the strategies of political marketers can be the solution to shift your mindset in the right direction. Throughout this book, you'll learn the details of the success tactics political marketers use on each and every campaign. I guarantee that your digital marketing firm does *not* want you to know the strategies in this book; they would prefer that you continue to believe the following seven lies.

1. **Lie: You must sign a long-term contract (and sometimes even fork over a huge signing bonus).** Digital marketing firms act as though the client needs to pay for the privilege of working with them by mandating unbreakable contracts of anywhere from six to eighteen months. Tell me: once they've cashed your check, what possible motivation do you think they have to do their best work for your business? In the following chapters, I'll show you a way to counter the contract and demand back the leverage in your marketing relationship.

2. **Lie: You have to spend big to discover what works.** Why would you invest big money on a marketing campaign before you know what will resonate with your customers, and what they'll respond to? In politics, we spend the tiniest amount possible in testing

of ads to know exactly what will hit the voters hardest *before* we spend a huge chunk of the client's money. There's a more efficient and effective way to ensure success; in the following chapters, you'll see how to get the most bang for your buck *before* you make a large digital marketing investment.

3. **Lie: Paying your marketing firm by the hour saves you money.** In politics, we work on a monthly retainer, and from that monthly fee, the client can squeeze every last hour possible out of us. In the digital marketing world, many firms are paid by the hour. Every time you call up your firm, are you mentally wincing at the $400 you just spent to ask them a quick question? Throughout this book, I'll show you a better way—how to build a stronger relationship with your marketing firm, and motivate them to do everything they can to work for your win.

4. **Lie: "Your product (or service) is *amazing*, so let's start there!"** So many business owners get their egos stroked by their digital marketing firm, and end up with an ad campaign that speaks more to them than to their customers. In politics, winning isn't an ego game—it's about converting voters to vote for our candidate. In this book, you'll learn how to build a marketing foundation around what your customer is already telling you, not what you want them to hear.

5. **Lie: Your firm is working hard to make you stand out from the crowd.** Marketing firms will *tell* a client they're highlighting their key unique differential to make them pop among their competitors—but behind closed doors, marketing firms are terrified

that authenticity will backfire. As a result, they work hard to keep their client's marketing generic and safe so the contract will last as long as possible. They churn out tons of content to create the impression they're working hard, but the content is safe, watered-down, and uninspiring. In politics, we work hard to humanize our candidates with authenticity and try to stay away from robot-speak, because the voters can spot inauthenticity a mile away. Success is rooted in authenticity, and the best political marketers lead the way on that front. Does your business communication sound more like gobbledygook than conversation? I'll show you examples of why it's more important than ever to connect with your audience in an authentic way.

6. **Lie: Your outcome takes priority over their payday.** In business, the mindset is all wrong—your marketing firm gets paid whether you win or lose, so how can you expect them to work for your win? In politics, we have no option but to win. Our mindset is wholly focused on that outcome. We don't succeed unless our candidates win, so we are conditioned to put their outcomes first. In the following chapters, you'll see how this mindset shift is the most important thing you can do for your business.

7. **Lie: If you brand it, they will come.** Most digital marketers push a "brand first, conversion second" mentality that brings in a good ROI for them, but not necessarily for their client. In politics, that thinking is reversed. In this book, you'll learn how to engage your customer and convert *first,* then use branding to reinforce your message and engagement.

The fact that you've even picked up this book at all is your first step in embracing this new mindset. To see the results you want, though—to revitalize and explode your business in this changing economy—you need to go all-in. This mindset doesn't just encompass marketing, it infuses everything that makes your business not just survive, but *thrive*—everything from hiring the right people to showing them the best leadership possible.

The disruption is coming faster than you think. Are you going to sit on the sidelines, or are you ready to jump in the game, take control of your business, and take off?

CHAPTER ONE

YOU MUST INNOVATE NOW

"Business has only two functions, marketing and innovation."

PETER DRUCKER

Four days before Election Day 2000, a story broke about George W. Bush that had the potential to completely derail his candidacy in the critical last days before the voters made their choice for President. The last weekend of the race, it came out that, back when he was thirty years old, Bush had been arrested for a DUI.

Today, most people who even remember this story wonder why we all cared so much. Back then, though, this was a really big deal. It wasn't just that, decades previously, Bush had been driving under the influence;

what made it worse was that he hadn't revealed this transgression before his campaign. He'd tried to sweep it under the rug.

Trust me: that *never* works.

I'll never forget those final days after the story broke the weekend before Election Day. I was backstage in Las Cruces, New Mexico, alongside Dick Cheney and his aide. We watched news reports on the breaking DUI story together on one of the TV monitors huddled backstage of the rally venue. Today, it would have been more like the three of us getting simultaneous phone notifications of the tweets and Google Alerts pouring in, but back then, it was a breaking news story across all the major TV networks.

I asked Cheney if he'd known about the DUI. "No," he replied. "I'm just finding out about it, too."

The question on all of our minds was how it would affect Election Day. Al Gore's campaign was executing a strong Get Out the Vote machine, and several states that shouldn't have been close were now battlegrounds.

"I'm sure it'll be all right," Cheney said, his voice less confident than his words.

I'll bet you already know what I'm going to say next. It wasn't all right.

Yes, Bush still won the Presidency, but it took a knock-down, drag-out fight that eventually wound up being settled by the Supreme Court, all because the results were simply too close to call. *Why* was the election too close to call? Well, polls showed us that the DUI bombshell definitely contributed to the razor-thin margin. States in which Bush had a slight lead—key states, like Florida and New Mexico—shifted over that last weekend from clearly in our court to hanging in the balance.

Florida became the final battleground in what had become an ugly fight. I, along with countless other political oper-atives, lawyers, and campaign officials, were shipped to Florida to help on the recount team. When I say this was a battle, I'm not exaggerating. For an entire month, our team *fought like hell*.

Our directive was this: *do whatever you have to do to block anything that's not a clear vote for Al Gore*. Gore's team had the exact same strategy. For a month, both Bush and Gore recount teams scrutinized thousands of ballots, and bat-tled over anything ambiguous. If a person had punched a ballot five times for all the Presidential candidates, Bush's recount team screamed that it shouldn't be discounted, and Gore's team screamed that it was clearly a vote for Gore. Remember the whole "hanging chad" controversy? Imagine eating, breathing, and sleeping hanging chads 24/7. It was war.

In the end, as you know, the Supreme Court ruled in our favor in their decision on *Bush v Gore*, and Bush won Florida, and the election, by a margin of 537 votes out of 5,825,043 votes cast.

(By the way: think about that insanely slim margin of victory every time you consider skipping the polling station line on Election Day—*yes, your vote matters.*)

It was a victory, but it had nearly ended us. In the aftermath, there was one prevailing thought. *We never want to go through that again.*

The way forward was clear—we needed to *innovate*. We needed to study what had gone wrong and come up with new, creative methods for reaching voters for the reelection in four years. We wanted that reelection to be as painless as possible.

We asked ourselves: How could we innovate to make sure we were *never* put in that kind of position again?

YOU WIN OR YOU DIE

Politics is unlike every other business on earth, but a political campaign is also like a startup business...on steroids.

On a political campaign, we often start with candidates who often have no money. We start with zero. We have to raise millions of dollars in a very short period of time, and then we have to spend every one of those millions of dollars in a small window of the campaign—usually ranging from ten to eighteen months. There's no growth capital, no thought of a future investment beyond Election Day. We raise money, and then we spend it all—to win.

This means that every dollar has to count. We can't waste a single penny. Talk about a lean startup mentality—if we deploy a strategy that bombs, we have to *immediately* pivot to a strategy that will be a winner.

We don't have time to talk in endless circles or hold days of meetings. We move swiftly because there is no other choice. Election Day is our deadline, and it's inescapable.

The testing that goes on inside a political campaign is intricate and epic. Every single concept has to be tested; every single audience has to be hit with a whole landscape of concepts to figure out what will reach the most voters the most effectively. We don't have the luxury of coming up with ten concepts—two or three of which may be winners, and seven of which will fail—and spending a million dollars to try out all of them. We have to perform microtest after microtest to narrow down exactly what will work and put our money where it will count.

The world of corporate and small business marketing operates entirely differently. When a business client signs with a marketing firm, they typically sign a contract of a year or more; sometimes with a costly upfront hourly rate. For the business owner, the money they're spending on their marketing firm is a total crapshoot. The strategy the marketing firm comes up with might work and achieve the business's objectives, but it also might not. The marketing firm gets paid out on their contract either way. The marketing firm can do what it usually does with all of its clients: come up with a spread of strategies that test a wide field of audiences, but probably doesn't specifically target any one audience with any efficiency. Simply put, there's no motivation to win, only the obligation to fulfill the terms of the contract and execute a marketing strategy.

After the 2000 recount, we took apart everything we knew about voter outreach and rebuilt our strategies from the ground up. Before 2000, Democrats had dominated "get out the vote" organizing for decades; the close call in 2000 forced the Republican Party to change, innovate,

LIE #1: YOU MUST SIGN A LONG-TERM CONTRACT

Traditional and digital marketing agencies often require unbreakable long-term contracts, which are set up so that they always win, even if their client doesn't (anything over three months, by the way, should be considered a long-term contract). Sometimes these agencies even demand an up-front signing bonus for the "privilege" of hiring them.

That's bullshit.

In politics, we take the opposite tack: the best political marketing firms think about the client's outcome first, and back up their work with contracts that always go month-to-month. If our candidate isn't happy with our performance, they can instantly end the contract. And if our candidate ends up losing, *we lose*, because we're out of a job (and we're less likely to be hired in the future). We prove ourselves every single day with the knowledge that if we're not on track for our client's win, we won't get paid.

and figure out a way to beat the Democrats at the game they'd been winning.

Out of the ashes of the "hanging chad" wars, the 72-Hour Program was born. This program focused on the last three days before Election Day, and everything that could be done to motivate and persuade voters in those final seventy-two hours. By the end of 2003, I found myself the National 72-Hour Director for the Republican National Committee and the Bush-Cheney reelection campaign. From Karl Rove to the operatives in the field, everyone imagined and tested everything that could possibly be tested about how voters are motivated to turn out and vote in the last three days of an election.

When was the last time you spent a year of your life focused on predicting, controlling, carefully planning, and executing what would happen over a single three-day period? Well, that's what I did; twelve straight months of work went into executing the 72-Hour Program. (Since then, political innovators have innovated even more—now, both parties have a structure in place that focuses on getting out the vote 24/7, all year round.)

Other innovations cascaded forth as well. In 2000, there wasn't much early voting, but by 2004, many key states were introducing that option to voters. We combined our 72-Hour Program strategies with concerted efforts to get voters to the ballot box early; we called it the "720-Hour Program."

The biggest innovation we implemented in 2004 was introducing analytics and data into our decision-making. Our leaders modeled the idea on the book *Moneyball*, by

Michael Lewis. We implemented micro-targeting, which allowed us to connect to voters on an individual basis about the issues they cared about most. Through the mad rush of research we did after the 2000 election, we found out that certain voters, who we called "soft voters," only turned out to vote when an issue they cared about deeply hung in the balance. Otherwise, they stayed home. Those soft voters could be the difference between carrying a state or not.

How could we speak directly to these voters? How could we even figure out what to say to them, that would ignite their motivation to get out and vote? We realized that if we combined the voter research we already had with easily accessed and robust consumer data, we could create profiles of voters and target the issues they cared about most. Then, we could micro-target those profiles with carefully pitched mailers, volunteer phone calls and door-to-door visits (remember, this was before social media platform ad targeting). We could speak to them directly about the issues that affected them most.

The Republican National Committee tested this 72-Hour Program strategy in down-ballot races around the country throughout the three years leading up to the 2004 election, and when it came time to deploy the strategy for the Bush reelection, we knew what worked. We knew, for instance, that it took an average of eight touches (think: receiving a mail piece, a door knock from the campaign, a phone call from a campaign volunteer, hearing a radio ad, or seeing a TV ad) in the three days before Election Day to turn a soft voter into a person who would likely turn out to cast their ballot.

The strategy worked. Our Get Out the Vote efforts were credited with winning reelection for the President, especially in the key state of Ohio, which Bush carried with less than 119,000 votes.

After this huge victory, did we go back to the drawing board again? Did we turn our eyes to the future, and think, *how can Republicans keep innovating to stay ahead of the curve?*

Nope.

Bush won, and we got complacent. He didn't have to run for reelection again. We were on top of the world, and from way up there, innovation fades into the distance.

THINK LIKE THE UNDERDOG

Just like a lean budget is a forcing function for creativity, being on the bottom forces innovation. That's why people bet on the underdog in a fight; they know that the underdog mentality is one that will do anything to get back on top.

After the 2004 election, we were so high on the innovation we'd created, and the massive win micro-targeting had given us, that we ran around bragging about it instead of figuring out how to innovate for the next election. For two years, Republicans walked around saying, "Don't worry about the midterm elections—we've got our secret weapon, and that's micro-targeting. We know how to figure out what issues people care about most, and we know how to motivate them to vote on those issues. We're going to get all those votes."

We got annihilated in 2006.

Now, obviously, there were other factors at play in the two years between the reelection and the 2006 midterms. The Iraq War spiraled; there was a fight over privatizing Social Security; the economy was starting to show signs of wear leading up to the 2008 crash. All of these elements, however, could have been addressed proactively and aggressively; all of them could have been dealt with, had we kept our focus on continuous innovation.

In politics, both parties are engaged in a constant innovation race. Someone always comes out on top in an election, and the underdog usually throws itself into innovating for the win the next time around. That's why party control over the government tends to be cyclical.

In business, the underdog mentality is what has created some of the greatest organizations of our age. Amazon started out as a joke in the bookselling industry; nobody considered it a threat to major book retailers like Borders and Barnes & Noble. Netflix started out squarely in the underdog category up against Blockbuster in the early 2000s, and by the end of the decade, Blockbuster was just a memory.

When you're the underdog, when you're the one fighting uphill, you're willing to innovate and do whatever it takes to get to the top of the hill.

When you're the one on top, though, you tend to sit and have a beer and watch everyone else claw their way up the hill.

SURVIVAL OF THE INNOVATIVE

As I mentioned in the Introduction, disruption is coming to every business in every industry on the planet, and it's coming faster than you think. You have the advantage of planning for it, of getting out ahead—and if you don't, you'll find yourself dead in the water.

Want an example of this disruption? Take a look at new innovations in self-driving car technology. It's well known that we are moving to an autonomous-vehicle society—in fact, my young daughter will probably never drive a car. These vehicles will be 99.9 percent safer that human-piloted cars, and I bet that in a hundred years, we'll be looked back on as dangerous barbarians for driving ourselves around.

There are numerous first-order consequences to this disruption. For instance, what happens to the car insurance industry when our cars are 99.9 percent safer, and accident rates plummet? What will happen to lawyers who make their living suing for those accidents? What happens to First Responder and ER nursing jobs when car accident injuries shrink to almost zero? Even governments will be disrupted by self-driving cars—city and state governments depend on traffic violation fines for a significant portion of their annual budgets.

To take it even further, here's a scary second-order consequence: if we're driving cars that are 99.9 percent safer, and accidents are essentially eliminated, what will happen to organ donations? How many people waiting on transplants will die?

These examples I'm giving aren't far-off future possibilities; they're staring us in the face right now. My friends in Silicon Valley will laugh at these examples, because this is old news to them. They've already moved on from this idea. The disruptions they're working on now are beyond your wildest dreams. What will happen when every industry and job in the world is affected by the coming tidal wave of change?

How will you adapt your business? How will you innovate to win? Do you even realize that your day of reckoning is coming?

The onus is on business owners to recognize that there is a fight ahead. It's imperative that the leaders of organizations understand the looming disruption and embrace the underdog mentality, and start to innovate to match the direction in which the economy is shifting. If you won't innovate, you can't win. And with the coming transformative shifts in the economy, just as in politics, you win, or you die.

EMBRACE A NEW MINDSET

Back in the year 2000, Reed Hastings visited the Dallas headquarters of Blockbuster Video to propose a partnership. At the time, Blockbuster's perch on top of the

INTERVIEW: DAVID MEERMAN SCOTT

David Meerman Scott is an internationally acclaimed marketing strategist and the author and co-author of ten books, including *The New Rules of Marketing & PR*, *Real-Time Marketing & PR*, and *The New Rules of Sales and Service*. I sat down with him recently to talk about how the marketing industry has changed, and where it's going in the future.

The fundamental thing that's shifted in the past ten years is that, today, the buyer is in charge. The seller is no longer in the driver's seat. For the past century, the buyer didn't have a choice but to let the seller take charge, because there weren't any other alternatives; that's been completely flipped.

An example of this is buying a car. Twenty years ago, as the buyer, the only research you had at your disposal was *Consumer Reports* and the car company's own advertising; you gathered as much info as you could before you went to the dealership and put yourself at the mercy of the dealer. You didn't have any tools to independently choose the best car and negotiate the best price.

Today, you can use social media to understand ratings, safety, comfort, "cool factor," and, most importantly, price. The wealth of independent research available puts control of the buying process back into the hands of the buyer—the buyer at this point literally has more information than the seller. The balance of power has shifted.

So many so-called "digital marketing" agencies haven't figured that out yet. They haven't figured out that you, as the buyer, have the power. They spent their clients' money on trying to sell customers on what will make the clients the most money, rather than focusing their ad campaign on the customers' desired outcomes.

The vast majority of agencies out there have come from a traditional marketing background, and are experts in *everything but* social and digital media. Yet suddenly, with the shift to digital, all of them claim to be fluent experts in digital media marketing? You can see for yourself that this claim is false. These agencies treat a client's campaign as an advertising problem, instead of what a true expert would do, which is create constant original content on various platforms and target specific audiences who are receptive to that message.

Digital marketers claim to be experts in the digital space, and very rarely is this true. They know *just enough* about digital advertising to con the client into thinking they've got things under control. Only when you dig under the covers and start asking questions can you discover the truth.

media-rental market was entirely uncontested; the billion-dollar company was the king of that particular hill, with no competitors in sight. Reed Hastings was the CEO of a tiny startup called Netflix. He met with the CEO of Blockbuster, John Antioco, and offered Blockbuster an acquisition price of $50 million.

He was laughed out of the room.

You know what happened over the following decade. Netflix, with its vastly lower operational costs and no-penalty subscription rental model, began to outpace Blockbuster's brick-and-mortar business. A huge portion of Blockbuster's revenue depended on late fees from customers turning in video rentals after the midnight deadline (who doesn't remember a night when they raced to Blockbuster to drop videos in the return slot by 11:59 p.m.?). Netflix's model made late fees, not to mention the very notion of having to drive anywhere at all, obsolete.

It would be four more years after Hastings's original offer for Blockbuster to acknowledge that Netflix was a threat to their business.

It could be argued that it was already too late, but in 2004, John Antioco saw the massive disruption to his industry written on the wall, and made major changes to Blockbuster's business model.

First, he did away with late fees entirely, and second, he invested a huge amount of the company's cash into the digital platform Blockbuster Online.

All told, the changes cost the company $400 million. Had

Blockbuster seen these innovations through, it might have survived as a company. Instead, Blockbuster's board of investors lost confidence in Antioco and exited the CEO in 2005. His replacement immediately reversed both major innovations Antioco had instituted. Five years later, the company was bankrupt.

Blockbuster's leadership failed twice to equip the company to survive the inevitable industry disruption that was already in progress by the time Reed Hastings offered Netflix up for a measly $50 million. John Antioco failed to see the cascading changes brought on by the disruption to the brick-and-mortar rental model; he didn't innovate fast enough. Then, when he did realize the need for innovation, and made sweeping changes, the company's leadership reacted in fear and stuck their heads in the sand, spelling the doom of the entire organization.

Most importantly, Blockbuster's leadership failed to understand two key facts about business in the technological age:

1. Every industry will eventually face major disruption.
2. In the face of disruption, the only recipe for survival and continued success is constant innovation.

Every day, I meet business owners who are paralyzed by fear.

Here's the thing: why *wouldn't* they be?

The global economy is changing faster than most industries have any idea how to keep up with. It's been called the "Fourth Industrial Revolution"—technology, and especially digital technology, is completely resurfacing the economic landscape. The speed of change is completely unprecedented, and no country, no industry, no sector, will be spared from the ripple effects of this massive shift.

As the owner of a business that may have no place in the new economic landscape of the digital age, how can you *not* be nervous?

We only know two things for certain (other than "death and taxes"):

1. The tidal wave of change is unstoppable.
2. Businesses that choose to ignore it, or hope it won't hit them, will likely disappear.

Business owners need to embrace the same innovation mindset to take that first step forward and shift themselves out of paralysis. The CEOs and entrepreneurs I meet who are stuck are usually completely preoccupied with tiny, on-the-ground, day-to-day problems in the operations of their business. They keep their focus there because that's not where they're seeing the tidal wave of change. It's safe, and by fixing the little problems, they feel like they're doing something. But the tidal wave still looms. It hasn't gone away. If anything, it got closer while they weren't paying attention.

In politics, we innovate because we don't have a choice, and at this point, the world of political marketing has far surpassed the world of business marketing when it comes to innovation. Political marketers have taken the concept of innovation and made it the first principle of every action they take, every plan and strategy they create. We have the ultimate deadline: Election Day. Politics is the most outcome-driven business in the world; if we don't achieve the desired outcome quickly, we're out of business.

Most marketing firms aren't outcome-driven, they're contract-driven. If the marketing campaign they execute doesn't achieve the desired result for the client, they simply move on to the next client.

There's no scorecard which on which they have to hang their hat. They'll brag about their successes, but you'll never know about their failures—and how many times they *haven't* delivered for a client.

In politics, our scorecard hangs in the public's view for

everyone to see. Think about the focus that creates to win for our clients—we have no other choice.

How fast would you innovate if your competition knew about all of your failures? More importantly, are you getting the same focused, innovative mindset out of your current marketing agency?

If not, it's imperative that you break out of the rut you're in with your marketing strategy and get into the political mindset. As you'll see in the next section, innovation often means the difference between survival and death in today's ultra-competitive and rapidly-disrupting business landscape.

CHALLENGE YOURSELF

List three ideas where your business should be innovating in the future. When you've identified the most important innovation (with the easiest path to implement), commit to taking three progressive steps in the next four weeks. Make it a must, not a should. Think with a political mindset. How can you address the problem, adapt, innovate, and grow the bottom line? If you committed to this, answer these questions:

1. What is your innovation and its ultimate outcome?

2. How quickly would you implement this challenge if you knew that you would be out of business without it?

3. What is the timeline to implement your plan after the first four weeks?

Bonus: If you're a business owner who implements this challenge, I want you to share your story! I've created a Facebook community for entrepreneurs, non-profit leaders, and marketing officers to share their outcomes, insights, success (and failure) stories, and advice. Go to my Facebook page at http://facebook.com/ceophillipstutts—the results you share will help others and build a community. And your success story just might make it into the sequel of this book!

CHAPTER TWO

EXPOSE THE MARKETERS' LIES—AND STILL WIN THE GAME

"Get clarity before you get cool."

KEITH J. CUNNINGHAM

Keith J. Cunningham, an incredibly successful entrepreneur and business consultant, has been a mentor of mine for several years now. I visit him in Austin every three months. He's spent his entire career studying and implementing successful business strategies. Keith has run many, many businesses. He's run small businesses and big ones. One time, I asked him about the biggest mistake he sees other entrepreneurs make.

"Allowing themselves to be *sold* on a product, rather than *buying* a solution that solves their problem," he told me.

In this day and age, with so many digital marketing strategies, ideas, and distractions, business owners often end up being swayed by whatever new cool shiny object grabs their attention at any given moment. They see something work for another company, or they hear about a great marketing idea from a colleague at a conference, and they think, *Wow. I've got to do that. That's definitely the thing to do.*

They spend a ton of money, and usually, they lose most of it. It reminds me of a buddy of mine, who recently walked into a casino, pointed to the limo at the front entrance, and said, "When I'm done gambling today, I'll be leaving in that limo."

Fast-forward five hours, and my friend was walking back to his hotel room alone—dejected and broke.

Many business owners see next to no return on their digital marketing investment. The smaller their business, the more the loss of that investment hurts them. Here's my question: why spend that money before you know if that strategy will work?

Marketing firms hired by businesses do run testing on

LIE #2: SPEND BIG TO DISCOVER WHAT WORKS

All smart traditional and digital marketing firms conduct testing at the outset of their client's campaigns. But most of them require huge testing budgets. They're usually able to get the client to cut them a fat check to execute a test campaign. Once they know what works, they'll propose another big spending campaign to execute on their findings. That's two bites of the apple and a win-win for the marketing firm. But what about the company they represent?

Political marketers have been trained and conditioned their entire careers to initially take small budgets and run campaigns that test and refine, test and refine. I would never consider spending a large chunk of my business's money, or a client's money, on a testing strategy. That's not only a political mindset, it's a mindset of preeminence, pure and simple.

their strategies, but at a stratospheric investment level for their client—nowhere near the level of granularity that will bring a ROI for a small business. Worse, the big marketing firms sell an even bigger bill of goods to their clients: they convince their clients to invest heavily for the testing itself.

Many business marketing agencies don't want to prove their strategies before spending their client's money.

Instead, they tell their client, "We've got to spend a huge chunk of money to test out what will work before we really rev up your campaign." They take a bunch of cookie-cutter concepts that have been used over and over, and they spend the client's money testing those concepts within the client's market. Maybe a few of those concepts hit. The small business is now on the hook to invest more cash into the marketing campaign. Their firm tells them, "Look—now we know what works. If you want results, you have to spend more money."

WHERE IS ALL THAT MONEY GOING?

In a scene from one of my favorite movies, *Tommy Boy,* Chris Farley's character, Tommy Callahan, explains to a prospective buyer why other companies' product guarantees aren't worth the ink used to print them.

Tommy: Let's think about this for a sec, Ted, why do they put a guarantee on a box? Hmm, very interesting.

Ted: I'm listening.

Tommy: Here's how I see it. A guy puts a guarantee on the box 'cause he wants you to feel all warm and toasty inside.

Ted: Yeah, makes a man feel good.

Tommy: 'Course it does. Ya think if you leave that box under your pillow at night, the Guarantee Fairy might come by and leave a quarter?

Ted: What's your point?

Tommy: The point is, how do you know the Guarantee Fairy isn't a crazy glue sniffer? "Building model airplanes" says the little fairy, but we're not buying it. Next thing you know, there's money missing off the dresser and your daughter's knocked up, I seen it a hundred times.

Ted: But why do they put a guarantee on the box then?

Tommy: Because they know all they sold ya was a guaranteed piece of shit. That's all it is. Hey, if you want me to take a dump in a box and mark it guaranteed, I will. I got spare time. But for right now, for your sake, for your daughter's sake, ya might wanna think about buying a quality item from me.

If you're a small business owner who has a contract with a marketing firm, I'll bet you're paying through the nose for digital marketing services. You probably hired the firm because they "wowed" you in their pitch. Maybe they brought in a crazy creative guy to show you how cool they would make you look, and they probably stroked your ego a little bit, too. Most importantly, they guaranteed you results. Unless you're now seeing a clear and measurable ROI, I'll bet you're wondering where all your money is going.

To contract a marketing firm's services, most clients are looking at a twelve- to eighteen-month contract with a high hourly rate. Sometimes they even demand a signing bonus. This is just to see what strategy the marketing firm will cook up for their business—leave aside whether or not that strategy has been tested, or has any prayer of working.

(Seriously, I've seen this *so* many times—a digital marketing agency demanding an up-front bonus just for the "privilege" of working with them. Can you believe that garbage? It makes my blood boil.)

I have a friend who's the president of a venture capital fund out in California. About a year ago, before he reached out to me, he wanted to build quick product sales for a company in his portfolio in order to attract new investors, so he hired a well-known digital marketing firm. To sign the contract, this firm required a $75,000 signing bonus, and an unbreakable eighteen-month contract. My friend needed to get his sales numbers moving to raise more investor capital, so he signed.

After six months, my friend had seen next to *zero* ROI. He was wholly unsatisfied with the firm's work and responsiveness. They were reactive to his needs, not proactive. There was no mindset of preeminence. He decided he needed to end the contract. Upon hearing of his dissatisfaction, and seeing the total lack of success of their marketing campaign, did this firm offer to improve the situation and try a different course, in order to please, and potentially keep, their client?

Of course not.

The contract had been signed, and the client owed them the remaining twelve months of payments no matter what. The marketing firm wasn't working for their ROI. They weren't working for the win. They were just working to fulfill the basic terms of service the client had signed. They thought of themselves before the needs of the client.

The retainer model is another key difference between many business marketing firms and the vast majority of political marketers. A political marketing firm wouldn't think of operating any other way; after all, they're driven one hundred percent by the *outcome*, because their client's

LIE #3: PAYING BY THE HOUR SAVES YOU MONEY

If you're a business owner, and you want to maximize the time and energy of your marketing firm, it may seem like paying by the hour—i.e., paying only for the time the firm actually spends on your account—is the way to go.

But charging an hourly rate actually causes your marketing firm to hold back on innovation. They want to make every hour bloat into five hours. They want to turn a simple decision into a five-meeting series that costs you ten hours instead of one hour. They call it due diligence, or point to being detail-oriented and meticulous, but really they're just trying to run up the bill.

Paying your marketing firm a retainer—giving them a flat fee per month and then engaging their work as much as possible—puts the power back in your hands. It forces your marketing firm to work unlimited hours just for you.

success is their success. Why would you want anything less for your business?

In politics, we don't have long-term contracts. We have open contracts with a thirty-day "out" clause. If, at the end of thirty days, we haven't honored our word and satisfied our client's needs, that client can and *should* fire us, and find another firm who can deliver. There simply isn't time during a political campaign to screw around with a strategy that isn't getting results. Even a few hours of lost time can be the difference between winning and losing.

Think about that. When you're entrusting a marketing firm with the future of your business, can you afford to lose a few hours, much less a few days? What is your expectation and mindset? If it needs to be changed or reversed, what are you waiting for?

Another key difference between some marketers in business and politics? Political marketers don't ask for or require signing bonuses. Why would we get a bonus before we achieved the outcomes our clients want and need?

Instead, in politics, we have *win* bonuses. We get that lucrative cash sum only if we win. And because we don't have long-term contracts, we have to prove our success each and every day we're on the job.

You may be wondering: how do we do that? How do we operate a political campaign on a lean budget, and only spend money that we know will produce a significant return and achieve the desired result?

We do what the business marketers don't: we ask our clients to invest a small amount of money at the start of a contract in testing strategy. We won't sign a contract until we test assumptions, test target markets, and test messages and platforms. Before we ask a client to invest big-budget marketing dollars with us, we test and refine, test and refine, over and over, until we know what works.

GET CLARITY THROUGH TESTING

It seems like common sense: if you're spending someone else's money, you should conduct lean tests before larger spending, right?

This way of thinking is anathema to corporate marketers.

A marketing firm would hear that kind of talk and think it was crazy. Why do any work at all without a huge marketing budget on day one? Why demand a small probationary testing period on a lean budget when they can just demand a client's big check firmly in hand?

Many digital marketers don't want their clients to know that they could conduct lean investment testing before spending their larger dollars on an ad campaign. These guys would much rather score their huge payday up-front, and then keep their client in the dark about their account. This sounds sinister, but I see it all the time.

Lack of transparency in a confusing digital marketing

environment allows digital marketing agencies to gain the upper hand on the less-educated client. *Leave it to us. We're the experts. It's digital marketing. We know what works.*

These firms deliberately create confusion and dependency based on this concept, rather than being honest, open, and proactive in engaging their client.

The client is left to wonder—and I've heard this from nearly every business client I've worked with, after they've fired their marketing firm and hired us—*Are they really working for my success? How do I know I'm not just another payday to them?*

A recent *Wall Street Journal* article talked about the lack of transparency on Madison Avenue. Marketing and advertising strategies are protected as "trade secrets," and clients aren't allowed in on those secrets. All they're shown is whether or not the marketing for which they paid so dearly has brought them the result they wanted.

In politics, there are *no* "spending secrets." Hell, we have to list every penny of funding and every penny of spending on a publicly accessible government website! It's completely transparent, laid bare. And when everyone can see where your money is going, you'd better make damn sure it's going to the right places.

INTERVIEW: KEITH
J. CUNNINGHAM

Keith J. Cunningham is regarded as one of the foremost authorities on business mastery. He's the author of *Keys to the Vault: Lessons from the Pros on Raising Money* and *Igniting Your Business* and *The Road Less Stupid: Advice from the Chairman of the Board*. On a recent trip to Austin, I sat down with him to talk about targeting in today's marketing landscape.

There are four main reasons why your target market doesn't choose you, even if you believe you're doing everything right to target them.

1. They're afraid to take a risk—they perceive you as a risk versus the product or service they already use.

2. There is a friction cost in making the switch. *Friction paralyses them.* It's why the vast majority of iPhone users keep buying iPhones year after year instead of exploring the multitude of high-end phones out there; switching to Android presents too much friction, and they're stuck.

3. Lack of differentiation—they can see the obvious difference between your product and your competitor's, but it's not strong enough to get them to switch. In other words, they can't see the difference that makes the difference.

4. Lack of certainty of success. They want to test before they spend—which is smart! It's not pos-

> sible with most products and services, though, but without that certainty, they're paralyzed by fear of getting burned.
>
> Your business may encounter one or any number of the above issues, and it's important to tailor your marketing campaign toward the specific issues facing your business, or it's not going to be effective. Here's the problem: today's digital marketers live by the "bathrobe theory." Their work is one-size-fits-all. But your business is not a bathrobe.

In the last chapter, I talked about micro-targeting, and how it helped us enormously in reaching the voters in 2004 and getting them to turn out on Election Day. Since 2004, we've evolved that strategy even further. Sure, we can use consumer data and combine it with voter data to pinpoint exactly what a voter cares about most, and then deliver that voter a tailored, targeted message.

In the most recent election cycles, we've drilled down even further to perfect not just the message being delivered, but the vehicle of delivery: the ad itself.

Social media has represented an enormous boon to political marketers, but it comes with a catch—the medium and mode of advertising on social media changes so swiftly that it can be difficult to create a strategy that lasts longer than a week, let alone a month. It changes so swiftly, in fact, that any nuts and bolts I could write in this book about digital advertising on specific social media platforms would almost certainly be irrelevant by the time the book makes it into your hands (so, I'll spare you). However, a high-level look at social media advertising during the most recent election cycle illustrates the concept of testing well.

Not only do the social media platforms constantly shift and change their features and algorithms, but users constantly change how they access information on social media. As a result, if you look at two voters who belong to the exact same voter profile, you might see them respond completely differently to the same digital ad. One, let's call them Voter A, may respond enthusiastically to it, and the other, Voter B, may ignore it, or even respond negatively. It's a crapshoot.

Or, I should say, it *was* a crapshoot, until we dialed in our testing strategies and started testing everything we put out with our digital investments.

Think of a typical campaign ad you may have seen on your favorite social media platform this past election cycle. Inside that ad is usually a clear call to action encouraging you to do whatever the ad wants you to do—donate, ask you to volunteer for the candidate's campaign, remind you to vote.

Maybe the ad has a green background and a white button that says "Volunteer." Voter A clicks on it; the ad has inspired its intended result. Voter B, though, ignores the ad. To test what will work, we'll run the same ad with a different color background, and another with the word "Join Our Team" instead of "Volunteer." We'll alternate pictures or make the text more or less provocative, all to test what makes the ad as action-inspiring as possible. Usually, in these variations, you can see what really strikes a chord with the voters and motivates them to take action by clicking on the ad.

For example, maybe our ad is a picture of the candidate in action, and it doesn't perform well. We'll switch up the picture to a seedy D.C. landscape shot (if the ad is anti-establishment), or move the text above or below the picture and make the copy more potent and targeted. It could be as simple as a shift from "Support Tax Reform" to "Lower Taxes for Families." Same message, different delivery, and with many voters, it inspires them far more.

The scale of variability is immense. We don't just test the same ad a few different ways. On a typical digital ad, we'll run dozens, hundreds, sometimes thousands of variations, depending on our budget.

We figure out what people click on. We analyze that data.

Then, we serve those voters exactly the type of ad they respond to best for the rest of the campaign.

It sounds like a ton of work, and it is—but the ROI can't be matched, and it means that every possible penny of the client's money is going toward a return. Every dollar is working toward a win.

Contrast this with what business marketers do: generally, they're not as concerned with the client's budget as we are in politics. Again, they get paid regardless, and that hourly rate ticks off like clockwork. It's not that corporate marketers *don't* do testing; they do. But they do it at a level that is often completely wasteful to their clients. They test, *and* they get paid handsomely before they've proven anything.

A great example of completely botched testing can be found in the story of a recent grocery startup, Bodega. Bodega was envisioned kind of like Redbox, but for convenience-store items; the startup would put self-serve kiosks of household items and snacks into office and apartment buildings, and "disrupt the mom-and-pop corner store industry." Sounds convenient and viable, right?

They failed, under a blistering tidal wave of backlash, for two big reasons.

First, they were accused of cultural appropriation by describing their business with the word "bodega." The crucial point here to know is that the company conducted tests on the word "bodega"—but they tested with the wrong audience. They asked Hispanic and Latino communities if they were offended by the use of the word, or if they felt it was appropriation. The response was a largely disinterested shrug.

In a *Fast Company* article, cofounder Paul McDonald said, "We did surveys in the Latin American community to understand if they felt the name was a misappropriation of that term or had negative connotations, and 97 percent said 'no.' It's a simple name and I think it works."

They went ahead with the use of the word. What they didn't count on was a different audience—younger, "woke" Millennials sensitive to perceived cultural appropriation—taking *huge* issue with the use of the word.

McDonald then said, "...it's clear we may not have been asking the right questions of the right people." (You think?)

The second major thing they did wrong was trying to disrupt an industry that no one wanted disrupted in the first place.

Mom-and-pop corner stores in big cities all over the country are called "bodegas," regardless of the ethnicity of their proprietors. Those small business owners, though, are a treasured part of most of these communities. For various reasons, people love going to their neighborhood corner store. They consider the owners of those stores an important thread in the cultural tapestry of their community. They don't want to see those corner stores run out of town. They were offended by Bodega's marketing campaign, which positively described their intention to, essentially, put beloved neighbors out of business and out of their self-made livelihoods. (Having lived in Washington, D.C. for seventeen years, I loved my neighborhood bodega owners, so I get the loyalty factor.)

In the end, millions upon millions of dollars of venture capital funding was wasted, and Bodega lost a huge battle to make an impressive splash in the marketplace. It was all because they did sloppy testing and sloppy research, and had entirely the wrong message. With the right testing and the right message (and a better name), they probably would have done just fine; after all, a corner-store kiosk in your office or apartment building lobby *does* sound incredibly convenient, right?

Many times, when a digital marketing agency has done its initial round of expensive, hours-intensive testing, they'll go back to their client and say, "Now that we've spent this money on testing, and we know what will work, you should spend much more money to actually execute our plan." Often, the client doesn't *have* more money, or is so despondent about the money out the door that they bail on the entire marketing campaign. That's when the frustration sets in, and that's when they get jaded. *Why are you asking me for more money? Where did all the money I already gave you go?*

They're left without the results they were "guaranteed." The firm, meanwhile, happily cashes the client's checks for the remainder of the contract.

Most digital marketers put the needs of their *agency* first. You're the client—shouldn't *your* needs come first?

THE POLITICAL MINDSET IN THE CORPORATE WORLD

When I started my marketing firm, I knew I had an edge my corporate competitors didn't have. The swirl and churn of political campaigns, and the lean startup mentality, had prepared me well to offer a more targeted, effective marketing service to my clients.

The greatest advantage I had, though, wasn't knowledge. It was *mindset*.

Again, in politics, if our client wins, we win. If our clients lose, *we lose*. We are all in it for the client's success, and their success becomes our sole and unrelenting focus.

When we pitch a client, we do it with the intention of growing *with* them. Their success is our success. We get rich when they get rich.

To this end, we actually refuse to sign a contract for the first three months of our relationship with a client. These ninety days are our "probationary period"—and we insist on it because we know it will force us to do everything we can to prove our worth to the client. It also allows us to build trust. The only money we take from them in the "probationary period" is a discounted retainer and a small investment into the digital marketing testing phase. There's no big payoff at the outset—no buy-in they have to shell out for the "privilege" of our working relationship. *We* work for *them*.

Here's a fact that may startle you: since I founded my firm, not a single company that we've pitched to has ever heard of a marketing "probationary period."

Not one.

Not one CEO I've talked to has ever heard a marketing

firm ask, "How can we grow *with* you?" and then prove it beyond just words.

They've never heard a firm say, "Let us prove that we can get you a win, before you invest in us."

This tactic isn't something I came up with to differentiate my firm, or to make clients feel like they can trust us without a huge risk. In fact, this isn't a *tactic* at all. It's the mindset I developed from decades of work in politics.

Say what you want about partisanship, negative ads, lobbyists, pork barrel legislation, right versus left—everything that exhausts people about politics. Yes, it can be exhausting. But, at its core, politics is about service. Politicians live to serve their constituents. Most of them do, or *try* to. Are there shady people in politics? Sure. There are shady people in business, too, and in just about every other facet of human existence.

I've been at this long enough to know that one thing is true: the politicians who are in it to be of service, who are honest, intentional, and have a genuinely noble purpose, are the politicians who rise to the top (most of the time).

The same goes for business. The reason my firm has been

successful is that our business exists to serve our clients, and to grow with them—to share their success.

Our "probationary period" of three months allows us time to explore the client's market deeply, and to test and refine, test and refine. We don't want to come back to the client in ninety days with ten generalized concepts that may or may not work. We want to present them with micro-targeted, tested, and proven strategies that we *know* will get them to their outcome.

Once we sign a client, we don't charge them by the hour like many marketing firms, let alone demand an over-the-top retainer that will choke the lifeblood out of most small businesses. We work on a reasonable retainer that allows the client to get as many hours out of us as possible for the money they're spending. We don't create ways to make simple things cost the client dozens of hours; we simply do the best work we can for the flat fee they're paying us, and we work as hard as we can to deliver results.

At the end of the day, their business is at stake. They're going to make an emotional decision. You want to make that decision as foolproof for them as possible. You want to work for their win.

You can demand the same thing of your marketing firm—

and you *should*. Why give them their payday before they've done the work? Why put your financial trust in them before they've proven that they're in it for *your* success?

Audit your marketing firm. Ask them about the extent of their testing strategies; ask them how they can prove to you that their work is going to give you the best results. Make them get creative and hungry with a limited budget. *Force* them to grow with you, rather than keep you in the dark, taking stabs, and hoping for the best.

And if they say no? *Fire them now.*

CHALLENGE YOUR
MARKETING FIRM

Let's see if your marketing agency is resilient and working for your win. Give your marketing firm a concept to test. Then give them an incredibly limited amount of time, and a bare-bones budget they'll need to squeeze every drop out of. Tell them that at the end of the time allotment, if the results aren't there, you'll walk.

Their reaction will tell you everything you need to know about their mindset. If they take your challenge and come up with a truly creative and targeted proposal, they might be a good bet for your business. If they come back with a high-level budget, or complain it's not possible, then you should start to suspect whether they're really doing their homework and working for your company's success.

If they refuse to take your challenge, well—you know what to do.

Bonus: How did this challenge work for you? What did you test and what did you learn? Do you think your story can help other business owners? If so, don't forget to check in with your fellow readers at http://facebook.com/ceophillipstutts.

CHAPTER THREE

GET OFF YOUR ASS AND MOVE FAST

"What we maybe should've realized sooner was that we are running a political campaign, and the candidate is Uber."

TRAVIS KALANICK

I have a friend and colleague who recently moved from a career in political campaigning to a career in corporate marketing. He took a position with a big marketing firm and dove in headfirst, excited to use what he'd learned in the political arena to help build businesses and strategize for their long-term growth and success.

On the first account he worked, the team met with their

client and tasked my friend with putting together a strategy memo for the client's business. Fired up, my friend sat down and, within three hours of the meeting, had written the entire memo, a comprehensive strategic look at where to take the account in the weeks ahead. He sent it to his bosses and sat back, feeling pleased with himself.

A few minutes later, he received a reply from one of the supervisors on the account:

Slow down, cowboy. We're getting paid by the hour. You don't need to write memos that fast.

He was told that they had a process in place wherein multiple people would read the memo and give their edits. Those edits would be passed around, discussed, and incorporated. Then there would be another meeting to discuss the edited memo. Only then would the finished product be delivered to the client in—you guessed it—yet another meeting.

We have to get five to ten more hours out of this memo, my friend's boss told him.

This was when, my friend told me, later, he truly knew he wasn't working in politics anymore.

HURRY UP AND SLOW DOWN

It's hard to imagine the kind of scenario my friend experienced, because the political world is built for speed, and conditioned to execute. It doesn't always work that way in the world of business marketing unless there is a crisis.

In politics, speed is driven by the ultimate deadline: Election Day. Election Day defines every move and decision political campaigns make. After twenty years in the political game, *fast* is the only setting I have.

These days, many marketing firms are intentionally designed and built to move slowly. The more hours you take on an account, the more hours you can bill to that client, and the more you condition the client to expect things to take a long time. Marketing firms rarely have deadlines, they aren't staring down the barrel of an Election Day, and as we discussed in the last chapter, they offer no transparency to the client to show what's happening with all those hours they're spending.

It's a system designed to bill the client for as much money as possible. Period.

Marketing firms create massive bureaucracies within their ranks in order to slow operations to a glacial speed. They build in tiers of approval, teams upon teams upon teams, to scrutinize every single tiny detail of the work being done. They're able to pass this off to the client as "due diligence," as being meticulous and detail-oriented—and of course those sound like good, important things, so the client doesn't think twice when a strategy memo that should take three hours to write and perhaps another day to approve doesn't come back to them until weeks have passed.

What happens concurrent to all this scrutiny and "teamwork" is a massive level of paralysis, another hindrance to forward velocity. When you only bring a few people in on a decision, you can make that decision quickly. When you expand that group to a much larger size, that decision now takes days or weeks to make. No one wants to make a move; no one wants to be the one to pull the trigger. The decision and all its constituent details are discussed *ad nauseam* until it's time to schedule another meeting with the client.

Clients who have been burned by digital agencies tell me that in most of the big digital marketing firms, there are *endless* meetings, and a huge bureaucracy. There are meetings to talk about having meetings. There's a whole lot of talking before there is action.

And the whole time, the billable hours stack up.

Who's paying for all that talking? All that decision paralysis? All those meetings?

The *client*.

The bureaucracy of your marketing firm is designed for exactly that result. It's designed to build friction. And that friction is meant to bloat hours—hours that cost you, the client, wasted money.

Here's why you should demand paying your firm on a retainer: you can utilize all of their time under one flat price. An hourly rate puts you at a severe disadvantage because your digital firm will see every minute as additional expense—as an opportunity to make money. More importantly, it affects *you*, putting you in a scarcity mindset. You don't maximize their time because you tell yourself, "Every time we call them, it's another $400."

You become reluctant to do more, brainstorm more, and push different ideas. You use your marketing firm only for the bare minimum. Is it any surprise that you see lackluster results, if any at all?

The retainer puts the responsibility for your most precious asset—time—back on your marketing firm. When a marketing firm is paid on retainer, a client can use as much or little time as they want. They can reap the value they deserve from their investment.

Ask yourself: how many $500 or $5,000 memos has your company paid for?

If the answer is even one, why aren't you moving faster? Why are you waiting to fire your firm, or demand better work?

To keep up with the ever-changing, light-speed shifts within digital media and marketing platforms, speed is everything. It's the difference between winning and losing.

SPEED WITHOUT SIZE

Here's how that memo story would have played out in the political world.

On a political campaign, there are strategy meetings all the time, because the game is constantly changing, and campaign teams have to course-assess and sometimes correct. After a strategy meeting, whoever is tasked with drafting the strategy plan will sit down and produce it immediately.

Then the political marketers all do something unheard of

in many corporate digital marketing firms: they get the candidate to sign off and immediately start executing on the strategy. This entire process takes only a few days—sometimes a few hours. There is no delay.

This is the only way a political campaign can possibly stay ahead of its opponents and come out on top. In politics, speed is the name of the game. Every extra minute you spend talking about the decision, every extra meeting scheduled to agonize over the details, every extra person brought to the table to weigh in, costs the campaign precious mileage in the race to Election Day.

Contrast this with many corporate digital marketing firms—often, they get bogged down by bureaucracy and with company egos trying to flex their muscle. This in no way benefits the client, and if anything, hinders the success of the client's account.

Political campaigns aren't hamstrung by endless chains of command. They're not stymied by a giant pool of decision-makers, each of whom has to give their input before a decision can be made. In politics, marketers understand that the most important decision-makers are the voters. We work at their speed.

One of my political marketing employees told me a

story that perfectly encapsulates the point I'm making in this chapter.

Often, in politics, we'll describe a campaign as "building the airplane while it's racing down the runway," which is always a super clumsy way to launch a campaign. However, what really illustrates how truly chaotic campaigns can be are when you realize you have a situation where you're "building the airplane while it's at 35,000 feet and quickly coming in on final approach."

You might never encounter such a situation in a corporate environment, but it's how we think in politics. Well, the story of building the airplane while coming in on final approach describes a situation that happened in a U.S. Senate race I worked on recently. This senator represented a state in the Midwest. We faced a tough primary campaign against a self-funding candidate. The U.S. Senator I worked with ultimately prevailed, and then on the Primary election night, when asked what he was going to do next, a campaign spokesman said the Senator would be retreating to his home in the Washington, D.C. suburbs. Not exactly an endearing comment, especially considering he was being hit for his DC connections and not connected to home.

Following the primary, the campaign infrastructure

essentially disappeared. They had spent nearly all of their money in the primary and only raised $20,000 the month after the primary. While all of this was going on, our opponents' preferred candidate dropped nearly $1.5M on ads to boost his profile and continue the assault on our client, the U.S. Senator. Our candidate's team countered with very little. As an outside advisor, it was incredibly frustrating to see—so we sent in a team from the national party apparatus to audit what was going on.

Those senior operatives reported back that with two months until election, the campaign did not exist in any manner, and our candidate was on path to lose— which would have been extraordinary, considering this was a Republican state, and it was a Republican wave year. I remember sitting on a conference call and using the before-mentioned "needing to build the airplane while trying to simultaneously land" and folks were shocked. How could a United States Senator just let the other side steal his seat?

In a twenty-four-hour period, the campaign was revamped with new operatives to run the campaign, and the national party kept me on the ground for the last two months to run operations, as well as managing a group of field organizers who had never stepped foot in this state. We had to overcome a huge uphill battle of winning back Republican voters, not get killed with Independents all with the shortest of shot clocks (less than sixty days).

In a corporate environment, no doubt the turnaround plan would have taken weeks, and required countless consultant pitches on best practices and strategies. It would be inconceivable to overcome the steep odds with a short window to put them back on the path to success. In this example, we went from nothing to an airplane built to safely land and protected a U.S. Senate incumbent all in less than two days.

THE DEADLINE MENTALITY

So far, I've talked about the ever-present deadline of Election Day that motivates every campaign team to work fast, work well, and work hard.

There's another deadline, though, that's almost as important—the financial filing deadline. It's so important that we call it "the first Election Day."

After someone has announced their candidacy for an office, they have a certain amount of time to raise money before the first financial filing deadline is due.

Each campaign, every quarter, has to file for the public record how much money they've raised, how much they've spent, who has donated to the campaign and who has been paid by the campaign. This report, as far as the media and the general public are concerned, is directly related to the credibility of the candidate, and the viability of their campaign. It's important to show a big number when you file your financial statements for the quarter, or you lose credibility with the media and thus lose a vehicle to communicate with voters, donors, and other media outlets—you're laughed out of the race.

The first big win for any political campaign is raising an impressive war chest of cash before the first filing deadline. It's a signal to the voters that you're the real deal. If people are willing to donate to your campaign, it means they believe in you. And when other voters see the evidence of that belief, they believe in you, too.

To the slightly savvier media, the ability to raise cash early on is an indication of the ability to grab the *low-hanging fruit,* as we call it. The low-hanging fruit represents the donors that any candidate should definitely be able to count on to donate: friends, family, business associates. Put simply, if those people won't donate to your campaign, you're probably not a viable candidate.

Essentially, the ability to raise money early in the race directly translates, in the voters' heads, to the ability to win. And people want to get behind winners.

A candidate is in the best position for success if they announce their candidacy well before the filing deadline. These deadlines are always on the financial quarter—end of March, end of June, end of September, end of December. The most advantageous time to announce your candidacy, therefore, is the first week *after* the previous filing deadline, because then you've got three full months to raise cash until the next deadline.

When I ran the gubernatorial campaign for Bobby Jindal of Louisiana, he announced he was running for Governor four weeks out from the next filing deadline.

How did we, his team, react to the fact that we had just one month to raise the same amount or more as his competitors?

Well, there was a fair amount of swearing, and then we got to work.

We had our work cut out for us. At the time, President Bush had just announced that we were going to war in Iraq. If you don't know who Bobby Jindal is, he is American-born of Indian descent. If you were around back then, you'd understand that the mood of the country wasn't exactly warm when it came to candidates that looked anywhere close to Middle Eastern. Plus, Jindal was just thirty-one years old and running in the Deep South. Forget the political climate of the time—that's an uphill battle no matter the decade.

We had one month to raise as much money as possible, and we had to compete with more than fifteen other candidates for each and every one of those dollars.

Have you ever walked up to someone and said, "Listen, I'm going to run for office. I'd like you to give me two, three, maybe four thousand dollars. You can't write it off on your taxes. All you'll get in return is a good government. Can you pull out your checkbook?"

It's an unnatural act for someone to comply, and yet that's exactly what we try to get them to do. Usually, people hand over money as part of a transaction. They're buying something. They're receiving something in return for that money. Say what you want about politicians taking payoffs from big donors in return for voting in those donors' interests, but 99 percent of the time, political donors are seeing nothing but the hope of the government they want in return for their money.

Raising that war chest for Bobby Jindal was one of the hardest things I've ever worked on. Bobby and the team hustled like I've never seen before or since. He built relationships rapidly, drove all over the state of Louisiana to talk to donors, sat in people's living rooms to tell them about his platform and vision, and our team did absolutely everything they could to collect those checks. Bobby worked fast, so we worked fast. Bobby worked 24/7, so we worked 24/7. And no one took a break.

When we filed our financial report with the state of Louisiana on March 31, we had raised more money than any of the other candidates in the race. We were rewarded with legitimacy—the media blew up around our campaign, and story after story about "the little campaign that could" filled the national press. We won all the credibility and all the attention. The momentum built. Bobby skyrocketed in the polls.

That one-month deadline sharpened our focus and made us move faster than any other campaign. That speed, combined with well-tested strategy that kept us pointed in the right direction, drove our success.

Speed without strategy is useless—and strategy arises from careful attention to your strengths, and to what distinguishes you from your competition. Identify the key principles that will make you successful. Allow those principles to point you in the right direction. Then *take off.*

FOCUS PLUS SPEED TO WIN THE DAY

You may be wondering how to reconcile doing things *fast* with doing things *well.* And you're right: in business, and in life, those things don't usually go hand in hand. There's a reason a fast food dinner costs a fifth of the bill at a fine dining restaurant; with fast food, you're sacrificing quality for the reduced amount of time it takes to get the food from the kitchen into your hands.

Going fast doesn't always mean sacrificing quality, though. In business, and especially in the startup world, speed is crucial to the success of a venture. Speed will make or break the future of a company. The trick is to be fast *and* focused.

Take Silicon Valley, for example, the ultimate incubator for startups, and it's the ultimate blueprint for how to go fast without running off the rails. Tech startups are all trying to beat everyone else to market with the idea of the moment. If they hesitate even for a second, they'll be left in the dust.

A great example of a business that had no problem

moving fast is Uber. When Uber launched, the time period between execution and market dominance was incredibly short. Uber's team didn't blindly flail into the transportation market, either. They started with a great idea, and immediately got to testing to see what would work and what they could start to implement right off the bat to beat other companies to market. They carefully tested their service with each of the service types they planned to launch: black cars, then lower-cost sedans, then food delivery. Now they're moving at light-speed into drones, helicopters, and other burgeoning transportation service options. The key factor in each service is the speed at which the company tested and implemented. Uber's model is to identify a void, test what the market wants to fill that void, and then move at a hundred miles per hour to provide it.

Blind speed will likely lead to failure. That's not in dispute. But often, out of fear of that failure, businesses slow themselves down. They over-scrutinize. They meander and analyze. They failed to act fast...or at all.

Billion-dollar companies are those that, when they were starting out, understood that they couldn't just be good; they needed to be great *and* fast.

Investor and entrepreneur Mark Cuban purchased a $285

million majority stake in the Dallas Mavericks NBA team in 2000. In the two decades preceding this purchase, the Mavericks won less than half of their games.

Starting in 2001, and for the ten years following Cuban's purchase of the team, the Mavericks made the playoffs every single year but one. They increased their win average to 69 percent of regular season games. In 2011, they defeated the Miami Heat to win the NBA finals.

How did Cuban spark such a huge turnaround in the performance of the team?

He used the startup mindset he'd honed as an entrepreneur. He treated each NBA season as a deadline-focused opportunity to work for the win—taking home the trophy at the end of the playoffs.

Cuban's changes extended into every facet of the team's management. He focused first on building a cohesive team that clicked—he got the right people in place to work for the win. He treated his team like royalty, too; the players went from being shuttled around on red-eye flights and staying at Holiday Inns to being flown on a private team plane to high-end hotels.

He focused intently on the experience of the customers—

not the hardcore fans who watched the sport anyway, but the casual enthusiasts looking for a fun night out at a game—by bringing them "behind the curtain" of the team and building a direct relationship with them. While most team owners watched the game from up in the owners' box, high above the crowd, Cuban put on a Mavericks jersey and watched the game down on the floor with the fans. Most importantly, he moved the Mavericks to a new arena with huge, top-of-the-line JumboTrons, and had crowd interactions highlighted by the team's production staff.

Most importantly, he focused on something I've drilled over and over: *testing*. Cuban was intently focused on analytics, just, as he would be for any other business. His team tested and refined, tested and refined, until they knew exactly which player to put out on the court at exactly the best moment in the game to score points. This focus on analytics was eventually credited with the team's 2011 championship win.

When Cuban acquired the Mavericks, did he hold endless meetings, do a year of research, and slowly trickle in changes to the team lineup or management?

No. He *took off*. Speed was the name of the game.

SHORTEN THE LIFE CYCLE

You've probably heard this statistic a million times: today's average American has the attention span of a goldfish.

This means that not only do you have to move at the speed of their attention span in order to capture their notice, but that once you've got their attention, you have to move just as fast to *keep* it.

Gary Vaynerchuk, in his seminal marketing guidebook *Jab, Jab, Jab, Right Hook,* wrote about the acceleration of the public's attention span:

> It took thirty-eight years before 50 million people gained access to radios. It took television thirteen years to earn an audience that size. It took Instagram a year and a half.

Thirty-eight years, to thirteen years, to eighteen months. When you look at it that way, it's not just an *acceleration*—it's breaking the sound barrier. And trust me when I tell you, that acceleration is only going to increase.

If your digital marketing firm isn't moving just as fast as the public's attention, how successful do you think they're going to be in working for your win? How far is the hourly rate you're paying really going? How much ROI can you really expect when your firm is still having meetings about yesterday's strategy when it's already obsolete in the face of today's shifted trends?

FAST AND FLEXIBLE FOR THE WIN

Recently, my agency met with the CEO of a very successful medical company who was at his wits' end with the marketing work he'd received from another firm he'd hired.

"We just had a horrible experience with them, and I'm completely lost," he told us.

I asked him what had happened. He admitted, "Well, to start with, I didn't understand what they were doing."

This CEO had heard that they needed to get into the digital marketing game, so he hired a digital marketing agency who put up a Facebook page for their business to get them five thousand "Likes" on the page.

"We paid this marketing company a ton of money," he told me, "and we got five thousand Likes, but I don't have any idea who half of them are, and I think the other half are fake."

I knew, without telling him, that the marketing firm he'd

hired had happily cashed his checks in return for the easiest task in the world: getting five thousand Facebook accounts to give a page a Like. None of those Likes were targeted; none of those Likes would be actionable; none of them would be viable leads; none of them would be past or potential future customers. None of that mattered to the marketing firm. All they had to do was deliver Likes. And deliver they did. Check cashed!

This medical company represents the *wrong* way to go fast, and it's something I see so many CEOs and CMOs, and even just your typical everyman small business owner do all the time. They hear they *need* to do something new and trendy, so they rush to throw money at a marketing firm that can do it for them. They don't find out if they're moving in the right direction before they take off at the speed of light.

In the end, they see little to no ROI for the money they've spent, and they're frustrated and jaded.

If you are hiring a digital marketing agency, does that firm set expectations with the client upfront about how fast they need to move. Do you hear something along the lines of, "If you're not going to move fast, we're not going to work with you. If you're going to be paralyzed by decision-making, we're not going to work with you. We're not going to produce $500 memos for you. We're not worried about our jobs; we're not worried about getting fired. We're not working by the hour. We want to move fast so that we can grow your company's market share and *win*."

That mentality of working with clients, growing with their businesses, should be the guiding focus in everything your digital marketing agency does.

You need to be just as confident in your marketing firm. Demand honesty and ethics; demand to see exactly what's gone into the hours they're spending on your account. Are they moving as fast as they can?

CHALLENGE: DO A SPEED TEST

Identify a marketing goal that you've given your marketing firm. Let's say it's 250 new leads or customers. Do the above speed exercise, but with the time domain of a few weeks, with an affordable testing budget.

With this challenge in place, how carefully does your marketing agency target your customers or clients— do they propose a plan to spray and pray, or do they carefully target exactly the buyers who are most likely to bring you revenue and word of mouth?

It should force your marketing firm to get creative with both speed and direction. Once they've written out exactly how to execute and achieve your goal on such a short timeline, make the decision to accept their plan or try something else.

If they just can't effectively move fast, you know what to do.

Bonus: How did this challenge work for you? Did your marketing team move fast or balk at this challenge? Whatever the result, I'd love for you to share it and help others: http://facebook.com/ceophillipstutts

CHAPTER FOUR

YOUR #1 PRIORITY

...AND THE FIVE-STEP PROCESS ALL MARKETING FIRMS SHOULD FOLLOW BEFORE SPENDING YOUR MONEY

"Most marketing agencies take the lazy approach: 'I just need to understand this product I have to sell, and create something flashy around that. The client is happy because their ego gets stroked with a pretty digital ad.'"

DAVID MEERMAN SCOTT

My firm recently pitched a company that had all the ingredients for success: an incredible story, a great product, the ability to market themselves well, and the money to spend on that marketing.

When we met with them, all they wanted to talk about was their app.

Some marketing firm had talked this company into creating an app for their product. The company had spent $65,000 on developing the app. It was a free download. It had been downloaded a measly 1,200 times.

Can you guess what their first question to us was?

You got it: "How can we get more people to use the app?"

They were blind to any other potential strategy, and they didn't want to talk about anything else.

We tried to talk about all the things that made their product great for their customers, and about the cutting-edge strategies we could use to market the uniqueness of their business (depending on the research needed to verify it).

They kept coming back to the app.

Finally, we got real with them. "No one wants to use the app," we told them. "You've spent sixty-five grand to develop a tool nobody is using. Meanwhile, you have a hugely marketable, unbelievably high-profile business, and you're fixated on throwing good money after bad on this app. Forget the app. Focus on what your customers want."

"But we spent money on the app," they replied.

"Your audience voted on the app. The app lost."

"But we spent sixty-five thousand dollars!"

This went on and on. They were so hung up on their investment and the idea of *having a cool app* that they were completely blind and deaf to the fact that their customers didn't want what they were selling.

I've seen this story play out before, with so many other companies. Marketing firms operate on trends. They pitch ideas they've already done, because they already have the teams in place to execute those ideas. They don't innovate, or look closely at a client's customer profile to target a marketing strategy to reach those specific people. They walk into a client meeting and say, "Apps can make your business explode. You should do an app. It could be a unicorn. Think of the possibilities! Now, here's how much money we need to get this thing made."

Maybe it's an app, or maybe it's something else—but I bet

most of you reading this book have experienced a similar scenario in the past five years.

The client, trusting that the marketing firm they've hired—on which they're spending a fortune every month—knows what they're talking about, hands over the keys, and hands over the check. The marketing firm cashes the check and then figures out how to make it work for the client. It doesn't matter to them if their plan might fail—what do they care? They just cashed the client's five-figure check and will slow-roll a plan, development, expensive creative possibilities, and cookie-cutter advertising strategies. Cha-ching!

Why would you spend *any* amount of money on an idea, product, or service before you know whether or not your customers want it in the first place?

"FALL IN LOVE WITH YOUR CUSTOMERS, NOT YOUR PRODUCT"

I love this Tony Robbins quote; it's the backbone of the culture I created my political and corporate marketing agencies. But many times, marketers, especially digital marketers, tailor their strategies around products and services, not people. They fall in love with a product or service, and create marketing that will showcase it. They forget that not everyone thinks like them. They assume that if they love it, everyone else will naturally want it, and they base every decision they make on that assumption.

This plays to the ego of the business owner, *who is* in love with their product or service. And why not? It's their idea. They've shed blood, sweat, and tears to make their business a success. I get it.

Here's the problem: sometimes, that blind faith in their product or service can also be delusional. Marketing firms know this. They play off of that delusion to create a sale for their firm, often to the detriment of what should be their first priority—making the sale to their client's consumer base.

They come up with ways to sell things—which, ostensibly, is exactly what they're supposed to do—but they often leave the customer out of their thinking entirely. They go to a pitch meeting with a client and say, "Your product is incredible. Here are the latest tricks we can use to highlight this product, and make it look as cool as possible."

The client, of course, is already in love with their product—it's theirs, after all—so they're flattered and thrilled, and agree to a marketing strategy that shows off how sexy their product is. (Like building a flashy app no one will use.)

When the above company wouldn't let go of the idea of their app, I asked them a simple question.

"How many people need to download the app for the investment to be profitable?"

They had no idea. "We didn't think about that," they said.

"You didn't do any due diligence? You didn't demand it of your marketing firm? You didn't demand that they show you exactly how many people would need to engage in the app to create enough business and referrals to make you sixty-five-thousand-and-one dollars?"

"No," they said sheepishly. "We just thought we needed an app...and it sounded really cool, too. Plus, we've seen other businesses do apps. And our marketing firm aggressively pushed and championed our idea."

In my head, I was thinking, *well, of course they were excited about it! They've probably delivered the same half-baked idea to the other businesses you're talking about, and cashed those checks, too! Easy money!*

This happens in politics, too, by the way. Occasionally a candidate will launch a campaign, and they won't understand that to win votes, they have to make their campaign about their *message*, not just about themselves. They forget that voters vote for their own interests, not because they like the flash of a candidate. They might be dazzled by flash early on, but 99 percent of campaigns built solely around a person, and not what the voters want, fizzle months before Election Day.

A giant Fortune 500 company can afford to throw money at flash over substance; they can afford to fritter away millions on trendy marketing strategies that may or may not yield an ROI.

More than likely, you're not the CEO of a Fortune 500 company, or you wouldn't be reading this book to discover ways to improve your company's marketing. You're working on a budget. You're trying to make every dollar you spend work for you.

You can't afford to play an ego game. You need to play a customer game. A client game. A profit game. You need to play for the win.

In other words, you need to think like a political campaign.

THE FIVE-STEP CHALLENGE

A political marketer's job starts with one simple question:

LIE #4: "YOUR PRODUCT (OR SERVICE) IS AMAZING! LET'S START THERE."

Digital marketers know two things that guide their work:

1. Business owners and leaders love having their ego stroked.

2. Business owners are confused and overwhelmed by digital marketing, and will do whatever the marketing firm suggests because they don't know any better.

3. Because of this, by pumping up the product or service before conducting research to find out what the customer wants, digital marketers will prey on business owners who are frustrated and fearful, and stroke their ego by focusing on the product or service and sometimes pushing CEO-focused ads that only appeal to the owner's ego. But is that what the customer wants? When this happens, the customer can't connect with the campaign at all, because it's not about them, it's about the CEO; and the marketing firm still cashes their check, same as always.

Don't fall for the lazy approach of fear and an ego-stroke—to see ROI on your marketing spend, you need to make sure, through tested research, that the ads are aimed at your *customer*, not yourself. It doesn't matter how much the ad speaks to you—does it speak to the people buying your product or service?

What do voters want?

It's crucial to understand the voters before we position the candidate and begin to build the campaign's strategy. We have to discover what's deeply and emotionally important to the voters. We have to find out what message will make them watch an ad and support our candidate or cause, or click on a donate button, or punch a ballot for our candidate.

STEP ONE: RESEARCH

We use all the tools at our disposal—the same data most corporate marketing firms use—to establish what the voters are looking for.

(Plus, sometimes we can use the publically available voter database available in every state—*not* something consumer advertisers typically have access to.)

Once we know what the voters want, we take a look at what our candidate is passionate about. We look at their platform and their vision, and we map out where their passions intersect with the voters'. We put together a comprehensive list of messaging and issues that the campaign needs to focus on to build relationships with voters.

Then complete the most crucial task: we define what success looks like and then we go to the platforms where our voters consume media to get our message out.

How many votes do we need to win the election? What's our vote goal—how many votes do we need to win?

It's exactly the same question the company in my above example should have asked themselves and their marketing firm when the app idea was being discussed for the first time. How many people need to actually use that app to make it worth the investment? What message will resonate with the consumer? What media platform are they consuming and how can we test it? How can we win for the client?

STEP TWO: DATA

In politics, once we know how many voters we need to persuade, we start breaking things down. We come up with granular voter subset profiles and messaging data for each, with key issues from our master data files that appeal to that subset most. We break voting districts down with these subsets and profiles. At the end of all this meticulous detail work, we have a step-by-step map of exactly who we need to convince, exactly what they care about, exactly how our candidate will appeal to them, and exactly where they live, what they buy, and what media they consume.

Consider this—would you go to a district full of high-net-worth individuals and run an ad for a tax increase on the top 1 percent?

It would be like Snapchat targeting ads to eighty-five-year-olds.

As a business, you must first identify which customers want to consume your message, which customers would be receptive to your message, and which customers want the product or service you're selling. That's the starting point—not the product itself. It's not about inflating the ego so the marketing firm can cash a check. It's about ROI. Anything else is fraudulent.

STEP THREE: TEST

On a political campaign, when we do our research on voters, part of what we nail down is exactly which media platform each voter profile looks at most.

Maybe for one subset—middle-aged parents of college students, for example—television ads are where their eyes land most often. But for their kids, the college students themselves, it is a social media platform.

An important concept to share right up front is that all

marketers should be screen-agnostic. Great marketers aren't attached to any one medium over another, even though we're in the midst of a digital advertising revolution; they should just research, plan, and execute what the data tells them to do, and go where the target market focuses their eyeballs.

For example, we know based on research and testing that voters in rural areas consume media differently from voters in urban areas. We know that, in South Dakota, voters tend to spend a lot less time online, versus voters in New York, who consume the vast majority of their media on mobile platforms. In addition to the values differences, the strategy is completely different for targeting voters in these two vastly different geographic regions—so we deliver content targeted to the type of screen each voter subset looks at most.

STEP FOUR: LAUNCH

Here's what this looks like in practice. First, we conduct research on media consumption within our voter profiles. We might see in this data that target voters in South Dakota enjoy the same reality show as target voters in New York—the key difference, though, is that the South Dakota voters watch that show from 8:00 p.m. to 9:00 p.m. on A&E, sitting in front of their TV, whereas the New

York voter watches it sometime the next day on Hulu, on their phone or tablet. With this information in hand, we adjust our spend to hit each state's target voters on the correct platform.

One thing that doesn't change, though, is the *message*.

It's crucial to offer a consistent branded message throughout each of the different media channels to which we deliver content.

Think about a dartboard. Let's say that each dart in your hand is a different media platform—TV, radio, mail, digital—and your objective (obviously) is to hit the bullseye in the middle of the dartboard, which represents the voter's attention. Each dart, each throw, is different, but they all have to hit the same bullseye to get your candidate's message across. It's that simple.

You'd never want to limit your game to one dart. What if you miss the bullseye? You lose. You want to throw as many darts as you can, and increase your chances of winning. A few will hit (think: conversion), and a few will come close (think: branding)—you don't care, as long as you hit the bullseye as many times as you can.

Now think of a dart player who blindly throws their darts

at any surface they see in the bar, hitting walls, chairs, doors, you name it. They sure put some style into it, like the kind of darts the pros throw—they put some spin on the darts, maybe toss a few over their shoulder—and the darts land solidly with a satisfying *thunk* everywhere they hit. The player is confused when they lose the game. "But I'm a great darts player! Why can't everyone see how hard I threw those darts, and how many cool tricks I did? I paid for those darts and didn't win!"

This is the mindset of the business that is product-focused, rather than customer-focused. They're shocked that they didn't win the game, when they were never aiming for the bullseye in the first place. This is literally what I see in almost all of the business clients I work with. I'm dumbfounded, too. These business owners come to me frustrated, dejected, and scared to play the game.

My advice to them is: stop it! Learn the game, be an active player, and by all means, play smart. This is your business—your life—so stop being manipulated by your marketing firm and shocked when the outcome isn't what you wanted.

STEP FIVE: CONVERT

Privacy is a pre-digital age concept. If a consumer has any digital footprint whatsoever, marketers know *everything* about them. We know their lifestyle habits, their spending habits, where they eat, what they talk about, and who they care about—and most importantly, where they consume media. In today's digital marketplace, hypertargeting is so incredibly precise that there's no reason not to learn everything you possibly can about your customers—and there's no reason your marketing firm shouldn't be starting with targeting as their primary focus.

But typically, they don't. Why? Because there's not an immediate ROI. Research and data cost money, and it's usually paid by the business at the beginning of the campaign. Most marketers don't get paid on that, so they don't want to incur any fees that aren't immediately lining their pockets.

For smaller businesses, there is no other option besides smart targeting if they have any prayer of standing out amongst the big names in the market. Take an example from politics: if I'm running a state senate ad campaign when there is also a US Senate race, a gubernatorial race, or a presidential race on the ballot, I have to figure out how to break through, convert, and brand that down-ballot candidate. I have to be smarter and effective—with a *much* smaller budget. That means direct contact with voters.

We go straight to the source with a message we know will

resonate. We knock on the doors of our research-driven target voters, make phone calls to those same households, we create free media with issue-driven press conferences, and create some great creative digital, TV, and/or radio ads that break through the clutter. We make sure that the down-ballot candidate can break through, be heard, and win.

The same goes for a small business competing in the marketing space with big-brand companies. If you're a small beer company, and your customers are served an onslaught of Budweiser ads everywhere, how can you break through with your comparatively tiny ad budget?

Small businesses need to have great creative, unique, and memorable offerings that appeal to a customer's needs, and build direct relationships with their customers to build brand loyalty, advocacy, and conversion.

Has your marketing firm done this for you?

CUSTOMER CULTURE IS COMPANY CULTURE

For business owners, I'm talking about a mindset shift. It's about switching your primary question from, "Why don't my customers want my amazing product or service?" to, "What do my customers want?"

By working for your customers first, you're working for your own success. By connecting with your customers and building your strategy from the ground up based on their needs and wants, you'll create explosive long-term sustainable growth.

Creating a customer-focused culture should be a part of creating the overall culture of your company from the beginning. The same principles apply to your own team. Ask yourself, *what do my employees want? What motives them? What drives them to be their best? How do they feel connected to our company's mission? How can we grow together?*

Mark Cuban did this when he revitalized the Dallas Mavericks. He asked his management team, "Where have our fans been neglected? Where have our players been let down? How can I turn that around, and create the best possible experience for our team and our customers?"

As I mentioned before, in politics, a campaign focused on the candidate rather than the voters is a campaign that doesn't last long. There have been plenty of times when I've gone in to meet with a candidate, and all I've heard from them is how great they are and how inspiring their story is. Nothing about the people they seek to serve— nothing about the needs of the voters in a district, state, or region they're hoping will elect them to office.

I never walk into a meeting unprepared; I already know what the candidate's voters want, even if they don't. There have been times I've confronted them with the information, laid out their voters' interests, and told them, straight up, "The voters don't want what you're offering. There's no way you can win with that approach."

Often, they reply, "Well, that's who I am. I'm not changing."

That's my cue to leave. And I do.

I don't have any interest in working for someone who's out to serve themselves, rather than the constituents they purport to care about. I'm not interested in losing.

In business, it's so easy to get caught up in everything that makes your business special. It's that *every* business owner thinks their business is special, and every marketing firm knows this, and plays right into it.

Is your marketing firm interested in making you happy to get your money? Or are they focused on making your *customers* happy, so that you can win in the game of business?

THE CREATIVE SIDE

Think of an ad for a product you've seen recently that

struck you as incredibly sophisticated. It was probably an ad for a luxury car, or a high-end smartphone—those ads are incredibly artistic and visually driven.

Now think of the last political ad you saw.

As far as *artistry* goes...it's apples and oranges, right?

Corporate digital marketers knock political ad makers all the time for running unsophisticated ads. But what they fail to realize is that the objective of a political ad is completely different from the objective of a high-end product ad.

There's a logic to the messages and visuals in political advertising. It's clear, direct, and to the point. It doesn't need to be deciphered or pondered. It's not cryptic. That clarity and purpose is much more important to a political campaign than sweeping cinematic images of people dancing in front of waterfalls, or what have you.

I don't mean to suggest that the visual isn't important—it is. But a pretty image shouldn't be the foundation of an advertising strategy. Instead of imagery, political marketers start with audience. They figure out how to convince the candidate's audience to support their message, and they allow the visual to flow from there.

Here's a great example: several years ago, my partner at our political agency, Go BIG Media, Brent Barksdale, was working on a Congressional campaign in the midst of the Obamacare debate. Other candidates were going hard on the negative ads, shouting about both sides of the debate. What Brent found when his team did their research on what the district's voters really cared about was that the voters felt like nobody was listening to them. They felt that their needs weren't being met, and that they were hearing a lot of rhetoric, but that no one was simply asking them what they wanted, and listening to how they felt.

Armed with this information, Brent created an ad called "The Donkey Whisperer," which was a satirical take on the issue (by the way, go to YouTube and search "The Donkey Whisperer" to watch the ad). The visual could not have been more simple and low-budget. It showed our client on his donkey farm, talking to the donkeys and acting faux-mystified when they didn't do the things he was asking them to do. "They don't listen to me," he says in the ad. "I've been talking to these guys forever, and they still do not listen."

The hidden message resonated with voters: *I hear you. You feel like no one is listening, but I'll listen to you, and I'll work for you.* The campaign credited that single ad with eventually winning the congressional district.

"The Donkey Whisperer" has been viewed over 2.4 million times and won national awards. It was raw, and it resonated strongly with the target voters.

In political campaigns, the objective is to place as many nuggets as possible about the candidate in the voter's brain before the moment they pull that lever or punch that ballot card on Election Day. That's it. The goal is to touch the voter's consciousness enough times before Election Day that they are persuaded, and vote the way you hope.

Political marketers don't always need to create artsy cinematic advertising, because they've targeted each ad to *exactly* those voters who will care about the ad's message. We use our carefully researched and tested voter profiles to deliver content that tells micro-groups of people something specific about the candidate's mission that will resonate with them.

With businesses, it's strikingly similar. The mission is to place enough nuggets in a customer's head that they convert.

Many times, corporate marketers would rather lump disparate groups of customers together, because then they only have to create one ad. And the more they can play to the ego of the client in pitching that one ad, the less work they have to do in targeting customers.

At the beginning of this chapter, I discussed how marketing firms often play to the business owner's ego by falling in love with their product or service, before understanding the consumer. This also happens when a marketing agency plays to the CEO's ego. They know that *everyone* wants their skills and talents showcased. They create pitches that are designed to appeal to the company CEO rather than the company's customers. They create a highlight reel all about the CEO; they tell the CEO that they'll be featured in the ad, that it'll be all about *them*.

The CEO is flattered and excited. *I'm going to be in an ad! I'm going to be a big star!*

CEOs have invested their entire lives into their business. It's no surprise that they're excited; someone is validating everything they've sacrificed and earned.

Let me be clear: I'm not against highlighting a business owner in an ad. I'll only do it, though, if I know it will work. It's exactly the same as when we have a political candidate make a direct pitch to voters in front of a camera (and you better believe we've tested it before it hits the air). So, sometimes, the CEO-feature strategy can work—but it should be rooted in engaging the customer, not trying to pump up an ego.

Marketing firms expect this emotional reaction. They count on it. And many play on an owner's ego to land a contract and up-sell their ads for huge fees before they prove that it will work.

The firm takes a ton of money from the client to produce a highly visual, artistic, breathtaking love letter to an amazing product and the visionary CEO bringing it to market. What they fail to do, though, is to include in the ad any mention of the CEO's *customers*, and what those customers want and care about.

Take a guess: how well do you think that usually turns out?

AN ADVOCATE FOR YOUR CUSTOMER, NOT FOR YOU

Remember the story I told at the beginning of this book, about our real estate client in Hawaii who'd seen their entire ad budget go toward an ill-fated buy in the *Wall Street Journal?*

They came to my firm so frustrated and jaded that they didn't have any expectation of a win. They just knew they didn't want to throw more good money after bad, and they'd been burned by an ego stroke.

We took a budget that was 80 percent less than the initial budget, and conducted our research and testing. We found that pockets of people with disposable income in California and Arizona would be interested in buying coastal property in Hawaii. Our research also found out that many military families were looking to buy homes near the development on the island.

What kind of campaign would we have run had we preyed on the business owner's ego, didn't engage the research and data and targeted the wrong market? We already know what the results would have been: one single lead.

With 20 percent of the budget of the original ad campaign, we netted the client over 700 leads. All it took was following the five-step process: research, data, test, launch, convert. The client is still our client, and our company is growing alongside theirs. Their success is our success.

A marketing firm shouldn't consider itself solely an advocate for their client's company, service or product. They should primarily be an advocate for the people they are trying to reach and impact. That's the focus; that's what marketing firms and businesses must understand. That's the outcome.

Many marketing firms fall down because they don't make

any attempt to understand the client's customer. It's much easier for them to simply try to understand the *product*, then come up with an untested, generalized spending plan and tell the client, "This is what you have to do." They're banking on the fact that most clients will be confused and have their ego stroked. Most clients will be satisfied with a pretty digital ad, or an ad in a major online publication... until they don't convert.

If you're a business owner, or work with a marketing agency, have you focused their strategy on you or your customers? Have you verified that they know what your target clients or customers need and want? And are you allowing them to do it or falling for the ego trap?

As yourself: has your marketing firm employed the five steps to successful targeting?

1. Research
2. Data
3. Test
4. Launch
5. Convert

Ask questions. Demand answers.

CHALLENGE YOURSELF:
5 STEPS TO SUCCESS

1. Take the five-step challenge to your marketing team and demand to see that they're successfully implementing it.

2. As a business owner, set aside your ego and determine with evidence (i.e., research, data, and testing) what your customer or client really wants. If you do this before you launch the campaign, you'll save yourself money...and heartburn!

Bonus: How did this challenge work for you? Did your marketing firm implement the five-step challenge to success? What was the result? Don't forget to check in with your fellow readers at http://facebook.com/ceophillipstutts.

If you're ready to jump in right now and take your marketing to the next level, flip to the end of the book for an exclusive gift! This $5,000 value I'm gifting you will be like pouring lighter fluid on the fire that is your business.

CHAPTER FIVE

NOBODY LIKES A ROBOT

OR, HOW TO HUMANIZE YOUR LEADERSHIP

"We would only do that which we loved over making all the money, over the growing. The irony is that the more we prioritized passion, connection with the audience, authenticity, all of that, we grew exponentially faster than any of our other companies had grown. It was counterintuitive and awesome all at the same time."

TOM BILYEU

Behold the following hilarious tweetstorm:

Just turned to History Channel. No history. I used to get

history. Why do we have such a channel when it doesn't do history.

I've turned to History Channel several times this weekend, always Pawn Shop. No history. Change name of channel to "no history".

I turn to History channel frequently bc I like history. There is never any history unless u r an antique dealer. Change name!

History. No history. Axe man Timber. Nothing historical. Back to FOX. Sigh. Suggest to change channel name.

There is history on the History Channel rite now. Tune in before they go to swamp man.

Sounds like somebody's ornery grandpa, doesn't it?

Those tweets were from U.S. Senator Chuck Grassley of Iowa. Among the usual announcements about his policy initiatives, event attendances, and commentary on political news, the eighty-four-year-old Senator peppers his Twitter with utterly human anecdotes and rants, which his 180,000-plus followers eat up with gusto.

Sure, he also gets his share of haters. A small but vocal

minority ridicule his distinctive shorthand and his daft-old-man observations. It makes no difference to Grassley; he is who he is, publicly, and doesn't care who has a problem with it.

In shrugging off the criticism and speaking his mind without a filter, Grassley has probably gained more true fans than most politicians or CEOs with carefully crafted, expertly tested—robotic—public messaging.

CUT THE GOBBLEDYGOOK

We are becoming a society of leaders that are afraid to show any personality. Every public figure, from elected officials to CEOs, is terrified of letting the mask slip for even a moment; they're afraid of the backlash if they accidentally say what they really think.

The more robotic our leaders become, the more we crave a fresh voice and personality, someone who speaks without a filter. The most obvious example of this backlash against robotic messaging is Trump. As divisive a figure as he is, even his most vocal critics agree that he has *zero* filter. He doesn't run his messaging through a PR company. What we're seeing is the real him, and his unrelenting off-the-cuff style is a huge part of his appeal to those who voted for him in 2016.

LIE #5: YOUR FIRM IS WORKING HARD TO MAKE YOU STAND OUT

Most digital marketers will do anything to avoid rocking the boat. They just want to cash their clients' checks. To make things easier, they often scare their clients into playing it safe, watering down any communication the business or non-profit leaders may put out. Then, they can spend all of two hours writing a gobbledygook statement that no one will care about, charge the client thousands of dollars for the work, and sit back and call it a day.

Voters can spot inauthenticity a mile away, and so can customers. Nothing repels them more. Does your public communication sound like watered-down PR-approved garbage, or does it sound like a real human being talking?

CEOs and business owners often feel like they *have* to cover all their bases with watered-down pabulum because that's what their marketing firm has convinced them, and they fell for it, hook, line, and sinker. It's a lie, pure and simple. If your marketing firm pushes this lie on you, don't fall for it.

When CEOs allow their companies to show personality and humanity, it goes ten times as far in building loyal customers and brand evangelists. Even if it's a small local company, a business owner who puts out interesting, memorable content—unfiltered, non-robotic—will rise to the top of customer consciousness. Customers love leaders and brands who show vulnerability and empathy. The CEO who can show that to their cus-

> tomers builds loyalty, and more importantly, builds
> more customers. Their business will build faster and
> with greater success, because ultimately, the customer,
> just like the voter, wants to buy into a story, not just a
> product or service.

Leaders these days are afraid to show any kind of vulnerability, but what they forget is that *vulnerability* is exactly what people want to see—because it proves you're human, and it resonates. People want to buy into a personality or a company with a purpose, someone or something, they can relate to. Take, for instance, the epic rise of TOMS Shoes. On paper, TOMS are pretty aesthetically uninspiring, if comfortable, slip-on shoes. However, the company's "One for One" ethos—each pair of shoes sold triggers a pair of shoes given to a child in need—had customers flocking to hand over their money when the company first launched. Customers want to spend not just on a product, but on an idea. They want to be part of something bigger than themselves.

This core instinct of voters and customers has been so forgotten by most politicians and companies that we just roll our eyes at most of the canned, rehearsed, gobbledygook messaging we see from our leaders. Whether it's good news or bad news, whether it's promoting a person or product, it comes across as having been strained through filters, conference rooms, and battling egos within the bureaucracy. Customers—voters—are smart. They see right through that. They don't want to be told what some robot thinks they want to hear. They want to buy in to something or someone real.

One weekend in 2017, white supremacists and neo-Nazis marched through Charlottesville, Virginia with torches to protest the city's plan to remove a statue of Confederate General Robert E. Lee. Counter-protestors came out in force. Violence erupted, and the situation turned deadly when one of the protestors was killed by a white supremacist who drove his car into a crowd. Before the situation in Charlottesville unfolded, ESPN had already lined up several announcers to broadcast the first game of University of Virginia's football season, versus William and Mary. One of their announcers was named Robert Lee. He wasn't a descendent of Robert E. Lee; he was just an announcer for the network who happened to be of Asian descent. ESPN quietly pulled him from the UVA broadcast and sent him to announce Youngstown State versus the University of Pittsburgh.

The reaction from critics was swift and fierce. Just about everyone, no matter their political views, saw ESPN's move as baffling and ridiculous, political correctness run amok. What was seen as a massive overreaction provided fiery commentary on social media, with the network called "pathetic" and worse.

The moment the criticism began, ESPN's CEO could have humanized himself to the public by releasing a simple statement explaining the network's error. Something like, "I messed up. Actually, it was more than a mess up, it was a boneheaded decision, and as the CEO, I acted like a bonehead. I got caught up in an emotional moment, and the decision lacked all common sense. It won't happen again."

How would you interpret an apology like this? Feels authentic, right? You probably would have accepted the apology, shrugged, and moved on to the next thing.

Unfortunately, ESPN didn't do this. Instead, the network hid for a couple of days, hoping the backlash would die down. When it didn't, they released a canned, processed, filtered statement that offered no explanation and doubled down on their decision: "In the moment, it felt right to all parties. It's a shame that this is even a topic of conversation and we regret that who calls a play-by-play for a football game has become an issue."

Really? They regret it becoming an issue? Then *why did they make it one in the first place?*

If ESPN had shown some humanity and admitted they'd made a rash decision out of fear, the amount of goodwill they could have built would have been enormous. Instead, they put out the same old gobbledygook, and people rolled their eyes.

Let me be clear: this isn't an isolated ESPN problem. It's a problem endemic to the vast majority of leaders operating in society right now, and you better believe it's filtered down to small business owners, non-profit leaders, and even chief marketing officers.

Above everything, people crave *authenticity*. They crave a human connection. We're a more forgiving culture than most people realize, but the fear of offending customers is so strong that most companies and leaders prefer to be robots.

ONE HUNDRED PERCENT RELATIONAL

Because of the way social media works these days, businesses need to create and churn out a *lot* of content to keep their customers' attention. Most businesses try to cover the widest possible array of customer opinion with this content—they create content for the lowest common denominator in an attempt not to offend a single person who may buy their product or service. In trying to appeal to *everyone,* though, what usually happens is that they *bore* everyone.

Most digital marketing firms are so focused on making money, and on perpetuating the deception that will make them money, that they rarely come up with strategies to humanize their vision and purpose of their clients' businesses. The primary intent of these firms is to avoid making an impact—to literally *be forgettable*—so that their contract stays safe.

In politics, marketers don't work on long contracts, so we constantly innovate, especially in showing the unique and human side of our candidates. We think about and execute on this every single day, and with every single public appearance, debate, ad campaign, you name it. We are obsessed with getting the voters to buy in to the product—the candidate.

Additionally, political consultants, marketers, pollsters, and other operatives live and die on referrals. They aren't out advertising ourselves and their firms; they build a client base through relationships, and the referrals those relationships provide. Those referrals are about one thing: reputation. *This marketer wins races. You should hire him.*

Here's one unique difference between political marketers

and corporate marketers. Political marketers understand the relational aspect of business so well that they're able to leverage it by crossing over into the corporate and nonprofit world. Political principles can and do win for businesses. On the other hand, it is almost impossible for corporate digital marketers to translate what they do into success in the political world.

They try. They fail. That's a fact.

When digital marketers from the business world try to come into the world of politics, they crash and burn. I see it all the time; a digital marketer will see a news report highlighting the enormous amount of money spent on political marketing, and they'll think, "$3 billion industry! *Jackpot!* If I can take in even 1 percent of that huge number, we'll crush it."

They initially aim high—for example, a presidential or U.S. Senate race—and they'll inevitably fail to land that big one. Strike one. Then they move to a smaller but still significant race, like a U.S. congressional campaign—but they don't break through there, either. Strike two. Then they try for smaller race in a state where they do business. But even there, they fail most of the time. Strike three!

Why does this happen? It's because politics is built on

reputation. If a firm hasn't run a race, marketed a candidate, or won (the key point), then most candidates will never take a chance on hiring them. In addition, these business marketers, with their mindset of cashing checks, get laughed out of the room when they pitch a political candidate the budget they usually get away with on the business side. It's so outrageously high that it's thrown in the trash can immediately. Candidates can sniff out their greed from a mile away.

With their tail between their legs, a corporate marketer might run to a bottom-feeder race with a novice candidate who doesn't understand how to win. But that candidate typically has a small budget to run the campaign, and, with limited resources, the business marketing agency immediately realizes how completely outside their wheelhouse they are. They struggle through. A race like that isn't paying the huge sums a larger or national campaign pays, so they don't make much money, and when it's over, they come to the conclusion to jump back to the corporate world, and never waste time on politics again.

On the corporate side, the focus is inward, on the *firm*— political marketers understand that their focus must be on the outcome. Their sole focus is the win.

RELATIONSHIP-BUILDING DONE RIGHT

There are some businesses out there that *do* understand how to be relational, and how to build a customer base on the humanity and empathy of its leadership.

Tom Bilyeu is the co-founder of the billion-dollar company Quest Nutrition and Impact Theory, and he's built a platform to tell his personal story and the story of his company's mission and culture wherever he goes. He tells the story of how he initially wanted to be a filmmaker, and had success after filmmaking school, but then had one massive failure and switched paths immediately to go into business. His mistake was that he didn't go into business to make a difference—he went into business solely to make money. As he tells it, he was miserable. He convinced his business partners to sell that business and put all the money into creating something that spoke to his passions, drove him to work hard, and excited him every day. This shift toward working on a passion project is what led to the creation of Quest Nutrition.

Bilyeu went into a market that was already flooded—the protein bar market—and he disrupted it completely by offering a healthier alternative made from better ingredients. When he tells the story of starting his business, he talks about his personal connection to healthier eating, about the struggles of his team in the early days of the business, and about how he made it his mission to build his factory in a struggling neighborhood and employ people local to that area to create jobs. He tells the story with such conviction, passion, and vulnerability that people don't just buy into the product he created; they buy into the story behind the product just as much.

I put this principle to good use during the gubernatorial race I talked about earlier: Bobby Jindal's campaign for Governor of Louisiana. Understanding that the mood of the nation—at war—was not especially friendly toward an unknown thirty-one-year-old candidate with a foreign name, we focused on the incredible story of his upbringing and rise in politics. We highlighted the struggle of his immigrant parents, who moved to the U.S. from India a month before Bobby was born. We humanized Bobby and boosted the perception of him as funny and authentic by telling the story of his birth name, which was Piyush. As an eight-year-old hooked on American television, he changed Piyush to "Bobby" after watching Bobby Brady on the *Brady Bunch*. Then we highlighted his stratospheric career rise—Secretary of the Louisiana Department of Health and Hospitals at age twenty-four, youngest-ever President of the University of Louisiana System at age twenty-eight, Assistant Secretary of Health and Human Services for Planning and Evaluation at age thirty-one. This branded him as incredibly smart and savvy, the kind of guy a state with a lot of problems needs as governor.

Bobby actually got some push-back in the polls initially for something we didn't anticipate—*he talked too fast*. We knew he talked a hundred miles a minute, but to us, it was a natural and endearing effect of his incredible intelligence. Voters, though, were annoyed. We needed to figure out how to make voters see what we saw.

In that gubernatorial campaign, the main issue on the table was the immense "brain drain" Louisiana was experiencing at the time. Smart native Louisiana kids were going out-of-state for college, and they weren't coming back. In thinking about how to endear Bobby's fast talking to the voters, we hit upon the idea that Louisiana *needed* a smart guy like Bobby to come in and fix things. We created an ad in which Bobby told the camera, "People say I talk too fast. But we've got a lot of problems to fix in Louisiana, and we can't move slow."

This simple flip of the narrative did the trick. Suddenly, Bobby's mile-a-minute speech pattern was a sign to voters of his intelligence and ability. The polls went back up.

It's so incredibly important to listen not just to what the voters—or your customers—are saying in the literal sense, but to what they actually *care* about. The polls told us that the voters thought Bobby talked too fast, but the polls didn't tell us how much they cared about it (and the answer was, not much). We took the feedback *seriously,* but not *literally.* In a contest of issues between Bobby's fast talking and Louisiana's brain drain, the latter was the more important issue by a hundred miles. So, we used a natural and personal affectation of the candidate to highlight the more important issue, and the ad spoke to voters in a huge way.

All throughout the campaign, we found ways to tell Bobby's story authentically and strategically, and it resonated strongly with voters. He was elected to U.S. Congress in 2004, became Governor of Louisiana in 2007, and eventually ran for president.

Too many business owners don't tell their story. Or, if they do, it's generic, watered-down, user-tested, and boring. They don't take the time to consider that their customer wants a reason to buy their product or service over their competitor's; the customer wants to buy into a story, to be part of something bigger.

Another great example of a CEO who just *gets it* when it comes to the relational side of business is Tony Hsieh, CEO of Zappos. The reason Zappos became a billion-dollar company isn't just that it made shoe-shopping easier and more convenient. Hsieh built a *humanized* company. When a customer calls with an issue, a human picks up the phone. That person on the other end doesn't just solve the issue—they would go to the ends of the earth to serve the customer.

Early on in the company's history, Hsieh knew he'd done things right. He was out in California visiting friends, and he met a woman in the group who asked what he did. He told her he worked for Zappos. "Oh, my God!" she gushed. "I love Zappos."

Hsieh asked her why she loved the company so much.

"My representative who I always talk to when I have an issue—she's the best. I can call her 24/7, even when she's not at work, and she'll do whatever it takes to get me the shoes I need. She'll do whatever I ask. In fact, I can call her right now and have her order pizzas to be delivered to this bar."

Hsieh's response: "Yeah, right."

The woman picked up her phone and called her Zappos rep. "Carrie, I need four pizzas sent to me. Here's my credit card info." The order was placed, and the pizzas showed up a half hour later.

Tony Hsieh had created a company that was solely focused on the customer. If you ask Hsieh today about Zappos, he says, "I don't really care about selling shoes. I care about culture."

Hsieh and Zappos didn't just revel in their culture, they kept innovating by instituting a radical new vision. Employees exercise a huge degree of autonomy; everyone is their own boss. It's a creative and passionate environment. People clamor to get hired there, but anyone coming into the company expecting a party is quickly disabused of that notion; no one can make it at Zappos just sitting back and collecting a paycheck. Serving the customer is everyone's primary drive, and getting results is the priority of that service. Everything they're working toward is ultimately in service of the customer, and is about humanizing the experience so that customers feel special and stay loyal.

New customers follow right behind current, loyal ones. They come by referral; they come because someone told them about the amazing experience they'll have. In this way, business must be in the mindset to be just as relational and referral-driven as politics.

Another politician I worked with is John Thune, the U.S. Senator from South Dakota. To win his seat in the Senate,

Thune ran against Tom Daschle, the Senate Majority Leader at the time. Thune's win was one of the biggest upsets in political history, and he was carried to the top by his overwhelming authenticity. Voters felt like they could relate to him on a personal level. Authenticity isn't just an advantage in concept—it produces results.

To this day, I tell people that John is the nicest person in politics I've ever worked with. He's humble, smart, caring, and has no ego. In South Dakota, no one refers to him as Senator Thune; they call him John, and he sometimes corrects constituents who don't. If you're a voter in South Dakota, that means a lot. It's authentic, honest, and humble, which is what we want out of our politicians. It's amazing that he's the exception to the rule, but that's what makes him so successful.

You have to make your customer feel like they know you and have a relationship with you. That's what builds their loyalty, and that's what makes them choose you over the other guys.

PLAN FOR THE MARATHON

I don't want to make this sound like success is as simple as flipping a switch and sending out unfiltered tweets rapid-fire. That's not going to instantly make your business more successful. The fact is, in today's society, everyone wants to take an instant "fix it" pill. It rarely exists.

What I'm trying to do is shift your mindset in the right direction. The only reason political marketers understand that they need to humanize and be relational is that, in politics, that's all there is—from the candidates to the campaign strategy. That's the number one tool we have at our disposal to win.

In talking to business owners, chief marketing officers, and even those in the nonprofit world, it's obvious how frustrated they are with digital marketing right now. You have to create just the right content to get attention, and you have to target just the right people for that content to be effective. And the companies whose platforms we advertise on change the rules on a weekly basis. Successful digital marketing is *not* done with a quick fix.

Business owners see the world changing; they see the shift towards digital. And the business owner is usually confused by the new mechanisms to advertise their product or service. They pray that by having their marketing agency snap their digital fingers, *voila*—they'll have instant success!

The old forms of advertising were more in the quick-fix

style: you ran a TV ad or a magazine campaign, and there was an instant uptick in sales, an immediate validation no matter the efficiency of the ad spend. Nowadays, those marketing channels aren't working as well, so businesses turn to a digital marketing firm and throw money on the table to get the same quick fix. And what do the digital marketing agencies say in response?

"There's no quick fix, no magic pill. We're going to test and target, and spend lean until we know what works, and then carefully deploy a strategy of trust based specifically on what your customers have shown us they want."

Just kidding!

It's more like: "A quick fix? Sure! Give us a hundred grand for a Facebook campaign."

The most important thing for a business to establish is a *direction*. They need to establish their mission, their purpose, and their culture. They need to tell a story that resonates with their customers that moves them to conversion.

Success isn't going to happen overnight. Building success through digital marketing involves many tiny steps that add up to a huge distance traveled. You probably won't

LIE #6: YOUR OUTCOME TAKES PRIORITY OVER THEIR PAYDAY

In business marketing, the prevailing mindset is geared toward the marketing firm making money—plain and simple. It's a mindset of greed, slow movement, not rocking the boat, and locking clients into safe long-term contracts, with little focus on winning for the client.

The political mindset is completely the opposite, and one you need to demand in your marketing team. Marketers should work for their clients' win, not for a big check they can cash. Political marketers' sole focus is on winning *with* their client, and it's the foundation of every aspect of their mindset.

Business leaders need to understand that there is rarely a magic pill they can take to launch a digital marketing strategy to their business with instant success. They need to look at digital marketing as a long-term investment, not a short-term cost. They need their digital marketing firm to think relationally, be customer-focused, and test and refine. They need their digital marketing agency to think about building a relationship with their customers for them.

see the result of your spend right away. But if you don't get in the game now, you're dead.

In politics, candidates face absolutely *terrible* odds when they launch a campaign. The odds of winning a multi-candidate political campaign are closer to zero than 100 percent; this goes up slightly if the candidate has established their name, brand, and relationships. It's still a coin flip.

If a candidate is going to raise and spend millions of other people's dollars, on the flip of a coin, they have no choice but to move fast with a tested message that resonates. They have no choice but to test, so that they know they're investing correctly. By the time the last month of the campaign rolls around, that coin flip has maybe gone up to a 50 percent chance of winning. On day one, though, it's always hovering around zero. The goal of the political marketer is to move that percentage closer to success every single day of the campaign. Political candidates can't afford a day of lost ground, or stagnation. They have to lean on all the principles that guide them—speed, testing, relationships—to get their candidate from zero to across the finish line over the course of the campaign.

In politics, we constantly say, "It's not a sprint, it's a marathon." We say this about campaigns that are fifteen months' long, tops. Every day is about winning. It's one long investment toward a desired outcome.

Business leaders need to understand the way the world has changed, and start to think of their marketing as a marathon, not a sprint. There's no magic pill—but there's definite magic in a long-term strategy that moves fast.

TELL A HUMAN STORY

Back in 2007, Delta Airlines launched a two-month print and digital ad campaign in New York and Los Angeles, their international hubs, meant to highlight Hispanic Heritage Month. The aim was to evoke in customers the warm feeling of coming home to family, and to celebrate the unique values and cultures of Hispanic communities.

Tell me: what does any of that have to do with selling airline tickets?

To me, it came off as vague, watered-down pandering. I had a better idea for how to celebrate Hispanic heritage—how about *actually celebrating a person?*

Instead of putting out press releases with broad, sweeping language that didn't inspire anyone but allowed them to pat each other on the back for their "focus on diversity," Delta could have honored the Hispanic families who actually worked for their company. They could have told one incredible story, and made Hispanic Heritage Month about the real accomplishments of a valued Hispanic Delta team member.

This would have accomplished three important things:

1. It would have cut the gobbledygook and showed their customers they're not about bullshit lip service.
2. It would have honored in a real and powerful way the work of a person the public could connect to.
3. It would have been inspiring to both customers and employees—culture on both sides of the sales desk would have been made stronger.

Perception is reality. This is an inescapable fact for those who are public figures. The truth, of course, matters a great deal, but what also needs to be taken into account is what your customers, and the public, *think* is the truth.

A great example of this perception effect in politics is airline seating. The last thing anyone wants to see as they trudge down the cabin aisle to their seat back in Economy is their elected official riding first class. Now, the most likely scenario is that the elected official got bumped up due to frequent flyer points, but that doesn't matter—no voter wants to pass their congressman in first class on the way to coach. The politician was hired by the voters to serve, not to get upgrades. This might not seem fair to the politician, but perception is the only reality that matters on Election Day.

Showing your humanity is crucial in engaging with the

public. Customers—and voters, too—crave someone real they can get behind.

One of the best examples of a humanized politician is U.S. Senator Ben Sasse of Nebraska. He continually wins points with his constituents and the national public for his commitment to his principles, even crossing party lines to criticize his fellow Republicans—including the President. He actively uses digital media to espouse his brand, but he never allows his content to stray toward the watered-down gobbledygook of so many other politicians. He's authentic and empathetic toward the voters. Put simply, he's *real,* and he makes people believe in him. This is a big part of why he's considered to be a top choice for a future presidential candidate.

Plus, he tweets stuff like this. How can you not like this guy?

> *To whoever spent your Sunday signing me up for dating websites: Thanks, but no thx. (I checked with my wife, and she says we're still good.)*

Make yourself real to your customers. Be someone they can get behind. It's the difference between a transaction and a relationship—and relationships are what will make your business thrive.

CHALLENGE YOURSELF
TO GROW YOUR BUSINESS
THROUGH REFERRALS

Bring your best decision-making team together and pose them this scenario:

"Going forward, what if our business only got new clients from referrals? Each member of our company needs to come up with two ideas for how we can grow our business through referrals only, with digital marketing or another outlet as the primary delivery method."

Another way of doing this exercise that will maximize your team's results? Make them write the question on the top of a notebook page (yes, I'm saying to write with a real pen and paper), and ask them to spend thirty-five uninterrupted minutes away from all electronic devices, just with pen and paper answering this challenge. (This is an exercise I learned from Keith Cunningham, and I guarantee you'll be shocked by what your team can come up with inside those parameters.)

Bonus: How did this challenge work for you? The political business is 100 percent built by referrals and we've built our company to maximize this strategy. But I want to learn from you. Do you think your referral ideas can help other business owners? If so, check in with your fellow readers at http://facebook.com/ceophillipstutts.

CHAPTER SIX

GO NEGATIVE!

"The strong live off the weak, and the clever live off the strong."

NEIL STRAUSS

Tell me if you've heard this one:

A politician, at the start of his campaign, throws down the gauntlet, holds a big press conference for the world to hear, and says, "On this campaign, I refuse to run negative ads against my opponent."

(No, this is not the setup for a joke.)

It seems like politicians are constantly swearing up and down that they're not going to "go negative," that they're going to run a "clean, positive campaign" and "focus attention on the issues" instead of mud-slinging.

If this were the case, though, how come we're all bombarded with negative ads seemingly 24/7 during campaign season?

As a political marketer, let me make one thing clear: if our client's opponent swears off negative ads, that's the moment we lick our chops and go in for the kill.

Politics is a chess game. I've been doing this for over twenty years, and I've seen all kinds of strategies play out on the national stage when it comes to electing a president to a smaller stage like electing a local mayor. I've rarely seen someone win without, to some extent, going negative.

It's not always about decapitating your opponent. It's about drawing comparisons that make the voters question our opponent *just enough*. If done skillfully—for example, with humor—a negative ad isn't a hatchet job. If done correctly, the target of the ad might nervously laugh at it and says to their own staff, "Can you believe they did that? What an idiot. No one will take this seriously." It takes a certain amount of time before they realize people *do* take it seriously, and the paralysis of fear sets in. They wonder what they should do, if they should respond. They decide to make some noise in retaliation. By the time they respond, though, if you're running a committed campaign, you're already running the next ad blunting their response.

You've put yourself one step ahead of them, and they're stuck playing the reactive game while your candidate stays on offense, thus continuing to innovate.

This tactic works in business just as well as it works in politics, and we see it all the time. Remember the "Get a Mac" campaign? Young, casual, hipster-looking guy explaining Apple product features to the camera, while an older nerd in an ill-fitting suit tries to counter with what PCs can do? These ads were everywhere back in the mid-2000s; Apple made hundreds of them. Nowhere in the ads, though, is it explicitly stated that PCs, or the Windows operating system, are *bad*—there's simply a comparison drawn between the two operating systems that leaves PCs looking like the inferior product.

Combine Apple's ingenious negative ad campaign with their concurrent innovations with the iPod and the very first iPhone, and you've got a recipe for launching their business into the stratosphere. Which is precisely what happened.

The strong live off the weak, and the clever live off the strong. If you can gain ground by drawing a comparison to your competitor in which you come off as the better choice, you should do it. This is especially true if you're the underdog in your market; going negative starts to look more like

David taking on Goliath in that context. And you don't have to choose only one competitor; once you decide you're going to draw negative comparisons, if you're clever and skilled about it, you can play the stronger players in the marketplace off each other as well—to your advantage.

GO AGAINST THE GRAIN

I want to be very clear: most business owners don't have the courage to implement this type of strategy.

But I promise that if you do implement it, and do it well, you will win.

Something to keep in mind: if your business has a Board of Advisors or shareholders, they are never going to want you to go negative. This goes back to their inherent bias toward the status quo, and the paralysis of fear. Simply put, most people are scared to rock the boat even slightly. They don't want to come off looking like the bad guy, or won't consider it because they think their business is successful enough. They're also terrified that their reputation will be laid bare if key distinctions are drawn between the company and its competitors.

They're not entirely wrong—after all, it's harder to hide your flaws when you're pointing out those of others.

However, where this fear really stems from is what I talked about in Chapter Five; it comes from the fear of showing too much personality and accidentally offending people. Many companies rely on canned, filtered, focus-group-tested, completely neutered messaging to speak to the lowest common denominator and avoid making a splash. But if you think about it, how does that make you different, make you stand out in your market? What is your key driver that makes you both relevant *and* unique?

The companies that live in that space, stuck in the status quo, will never break out the way Apple did, or rise to the success of a smaller company that's willing to show some humanity.

When Apple launched its "Get a Mac" campaign, what did they have to lose? They were the underdog in that particular market, and they had the unbelievable benefit of being led by one of the greatest innovators of our time, Steve Jobs. Jobs saw that the vast majority of the market belonged to PCs, because PCs were considered "business machines," and Macs were "for artists." The only way to break out and put the PC market on the defensive was to "go negative," and draw the obvious comparisons not just in function and feature set, but in the very personality of the product's average user. The genius of the "Get a Mac" campaign was not that it pitted PC versus Mac, but that,

at its core, it pitted old versus new, stodgy versus hip...
uncool versus cool. At the end of the day, everyone wants
to be cool. Customers who watched the ads saw a vision
of Apple as the cool kids' table, and they wanted to join it.

In launching this campaign, however, Apple wasn't just
throwing anything at the wall to see what stuck. In entirety,
hundreds of Get a Mac ads were produced, but less than
ninety were ever broadcast. Steve Jobs was careful and
meticulous about which ads went out to the public—he
chose ones that were subtle, implicit, comparison-based
rather than overt.

Before the campaign launched, Apple had seen a dip in
sales throughout 2005 and 2006. Just one month into the
campaign, the company had sold 200,000 more Macs
than usual, and Apple ended the year with a 39 percent
increase in overall sales.

THE OTHER SIDE ISN'T BAD—YOUR SIDE IS JUST BETTER

A few years ago, I was the digital marketing and strategy consultant for a congressional candidate who had
enough money to start up a campaign and not much
beyond that. We needed to make a splash early to get
him in the game.

We were the underdog going in. When I say "underdog," I don't mean we were number two out of two candidates; this was a candidate field of *six*, and we were number six. We had zero brand-name recognition—literally zero.

We knew immediately that we would need to go negative to make our candidate stand out, but it would be idiotically inefficient, not to mention unaffordable, to go after each opponent one by one. With limited funds, and next to no visibility, we decided that the best way to go negative was to lump all the opposing candidates together as one, and paint a picture of our client versus the whole group of them.

Again, when you have a small budget and short timeline, you have to innovate. You have to get creative. So we did.

We created a vision of our campaign as our client versus the "gang of five." We tarred all our opponents with the same brush, creating them as a unified "other" group that we could pit against our candidate. We pointed out each of our opponents' inconsistencies on tax cuts and healthcare, and how our candidate was the only one who they could trust on those issues. We defined our opponents months before they defined our client.

At first, because we were the last-place underdog in the race, all our opponents laughed at our strategy. We were mocked soundly in the press. Then, as more ads started running, our opponents got confused. *Where is this coming from? Why are they doing this? This guy is in last place; ignore him.*

The paralysis of fear had set in with our competition, and meanwhile, we were still full steam ahead.

Instead of reacting to our barrage of Gang of Five ads, our opponents did the first thing politicians usually think of doing: they ran some polls and tried to validate their opinion that we were full of shit and our campaign was a joke. The trouble was, these polls came back with data that showed that we were on a trajectory to win the whole race.

Our no-name candidate, with a small start-up budget, shot from dead last to first place within two months.

This is the point where our opponents realized they needed to take action and respond, and by that point, we were four months into a five-month race. We had gone from the underdog to the cusp of an upset.

WHEN GOLIATH BRINGS HIMSELF DOWN

When you "go negative," you're on the offense, looking to put your opponent on the ropes—looking to make them defend themselves. Most of the time, by the time they react, it's too late, and you've moved on. They've been permanently weakened. Sometimes, though, the defensive reaction is spectacularly ill-conceived, and your opponent does all the hard work for you—they self-sabotage, and it can be fatal.

If you think Mac versus PC was an ad war, think back a little further to the 1980s, and the era of the "cola wars." Coca-Cola had always been the leader in the U.S. and international markets, and had easily outsold its closest competitor, Pepsi, since the 1950s. By the time the 1980s hit, Pepsi was willing to try comparison-based "negative" ads in an effort to gain ground in the U.S.

Pepsi came up with an ad campaign that was, in many ways, a spiritual predecessor to "Get a Mac;" they used celebrity spokespeople and current pop music to position themselves as the cola for the younger crowd, then subtly poked fun at Coke for being the "older generation's cola." It was a hugely successful campaign, and all it did was set up a paradigm of young versus old, then continually and frequently draw from that well.

Pepsi also used physical comparison to its advantage. The company came up with the "Pepsi Challenge," and filmed the public constantly choosing the sweeter Pepsi in a blind taste test of the two colas. Again, they never came out and said something overt like, "Coke is bad!" They merely set up a situation where any comparison would put them on top.

A few years into the 1980s, Coca-Cola had lost its majority share of the cola market, hammered by Pepsi's negative ads. They were squarely on the defensive, and they spun out in the craziest, potentially stupidest, most disastrous fear-based reaction of all time.

Remember New Coke?

If you are old enough to remember it, but can only remember it very faintly, you can't really be blamed, because New Coke was on and off shelves so quickly that if you blinked, you missed it. Coca-Cola spent all its attention—and $4 million in development funding—to create a new cola that would consistently beat Pepsi in the Pepsi Challenge. According to the reportedly 100,000 people they tested in their market research, they were wildly successful in meeting this goal; they did indeed come up with a new cola that consistently beat both Pepsi and Original Coke in blind taste tests, one that was sweeter, much more similar to Pepsi, and more appealing to younger consumers. Done deal, right?

Then they launched New Coke, and their world came crashing down.

Coca-Cola fielded millions of angry calls and letters from people who wondered what the hell had happened to their favorite drink. They forgot an important point about blind taste tests: *context matters*. If the participants had known that their choice of New Coke over Original Coke meant that they couldn't have Original Coke anymore, there's no way they would have been as enthusiastic about New Coke. Coca-Cola lost sight of the critical importance of heavy and super-heavy purchasers of soft drinks, who are the top consumers of the product. In doing so, they alienated their own heavy and super-heavy users, mostly blue-collar men who drank multiple cans of Coke every day.

There was a national outcry, and the media started hammering them hard with "they blew it" stories. In just three months, Coca-Cola pulled all New Coke from shelves nationwide and replaced it with regular Coke in the familiar Coca-Cola branded can.

The company was left with $30 million in unusable inventory, and a heavily beaten reputation. Pepsi didn't have to lift a finger—their competitor had self-immolated spectacularly.

The decision by Coca-Cola to research and develop a new flavor of their own product was, in the first place, a reactive measure. It was a decision born in the fear of losing market share to Pepsi's "young versus old" onslaught. It almost cost Coca-Cola their company.

Going negative, when done exactly right, costs you very little, and can cost your competition the whole ball game.

GOING NEGATIVE IS LEAN AND AMPLIFIES YOUR MEGAPHONE

To run a negative campaign, you don't need a lot of money. You don't need to outspend your competitor. You only need to outthink them.

One of the partners at my political marketing firm used a simple tactic once at the start of a political campaign when he needed to drum up name recognition for his client/candidate who lacked the resources to be competitive at the beginning of the campaign. He identified the neighborhoods where the opposing candidate lived, and he sent negative attack mailers and targeted geo-fenced digital ads directly to the friends, neighbors, relatives, and donors of that political opponent. It's the most precise of micro-targets, and it cost around $3,000. The reach was incredibly small, but it was a precision strike, and the amplification was massive.

When the mailer and digital ads hit, the friends, donors, and neighbors immediately called up that opposing candidate and warned him that he'd been attacked; just like clockwork, the opponent responded by holding a press conference condemning the attack. The press picked up the story. It became a huge story, and was instant name recognition and credibility for our client. As my partner put it, "Our newfound stature gave us huge name ID presence, and then helped us raise money and momentum, and we ultimately ended up winning the race not because of the inexpensive negative ad strategy, but because we used it initially to give our candidate momentum, and it worked. Our opponent walked right into the trap we had set up for him. We were playing chess while our competition played checkers."

For around $3,000, they elicited a reaction from the candidate that sets the wheels in motion.

You don't need to outspend your opponent on the ads themselves, and you certainly don't need to spend a great deal of money on background when it comes to negative ads. Sure, we conduct opposition research on every candidate in the field; sure, oftentimes some juicy details are brought to light as a result. But most of the time, the juiciest details are right there in the opposition's voting record.

We live in politically turbulent times, and if we're going after an opponent who's been in politics a while, there's bound to be something in their past, or even their present, that can be used to win for our clients, no matter which party they're from.

Recently, I worked on a U.S. Senate race that was the latest in a long line of difficult and close Senate races in 2012 and 2014. We'd seen that incumbents were in an especially perilous position. Our candidate was an incumbent, running against an upstart. We were at a disadvantage.

Luckily, our opponent in the race essentially did all our own opposition work for us, just by going about his usual business. Early in the race, he gave a speech to a local club about a hot-button issue that was probably better left unsaid. It wasn't a campaign speech, and it was early enough in the process that he probably didn't even consider it a speech the voters would know or care about. He just so happened to be running in a state where this issue was toxic.

Our side got a hold of the recording of his speech. We spent ten thousand dollars—pocket change, in the grand scheme of advertising—to create a simple yet devastatingly effective pair of attack ads centering on our opponent's missteps. We put the ad on YouTube and targeted it specifically to known primary voters in the opponent's state in five media markets.

The ad was released in early February and got more than 750,000 views. There are *not* that many primary voters in this particular state; voters re-watched the ad multiple times. It had a huge effect. Our opponent's favorable rating plummeted, and his unfavorable rating skyrocketed; by February 23, his unfavorables had increased by 233 percent. Almost before our opponent even realized he was running, he'd lost his state's primary, and his campaign was over. We crushed him.

Creativity is key in constructing a negative ad strategy—again, it's not about simply coming out swinging and lopping the head off your competitors. That would be dumb. The best negative ads are highly innovative and make use of social factors that will help spur the spread of publicity.

Sometimes two businesses can collaborate with a "going negative" strategy in such a unique way that it creates thousands, if not millions, of dollars in free marketing, and doesn't negatively impact the company.

Take the example of Moe's Original Bar B Que and Chick-fil-A. Recently, in Mobile, Alabama, these two chains entered into a spitting contest on the marquee boards outside adjoining restaurants.

It started when Chick-fil-A announced a new Smokehouse BBQ Sandwich on its marquee board. Moe's fired back with a response:

Chick-fil-A

I thought we were friends

Open Sundays

The last bit was a jab, referring to Chick-fil-A's famous adherence to closing up shop Sundays, as the day of rest.

Chick-fil-A responded on its marquee board:

Moe's we miss you!

Let's be friends again!

Moe's responded with a curt reference to their new best friend, the "gentleman's club" down the street:

Chick-fil-A I'm with Diamonds now...

But it would be my pleasure

Diamonds joined in the fun (and free publicity, as, at this point, the feud had gone viral and was being shared thousands of times across social media platforms on their own marquee board:

Let her go, Moe

The "feud" escalated until Chick-fil-A asked for Moe's famous white barbeque sauce recipe, and Moe responded:

Shyeah, we'll send it over

When pigs fly

The marquee signs were photographed daily, and the collection of all the signs in the chain of conversation was eventually posted on the Facebook page for Moe's Bar B Que. It was shared over seven thousand times, and the amount of Likes it received was exponentially greater, rippling out into the public with each share.

Moe's Bar B Que engineered a situation in which they were sure to receive the *best* kind of free publicity. It was the kind of exposure and goodwill from the amused public that a company couldn't buy with a million dollars in ads.

Going negative is one of the most powerful tools in the underdog's arsenal, precisely because of how little it costs. You don't have to spend a significant portion of your marketing budget on implementing this strategy; you don't even have to scale your attack to the size of the campaign. Done well, a tiny, micro-targeted negative strategy pulled off for peanuts can have a greater effect than all the rest of your marketing efforts combined, and the only resource you need to bring to the table in spades is creativity.

IF IT DIDN'T WORK, WE WOULDN'T DO IT

Being in the business of political marketing, I hear the same thing all the time.

"I hate those negative campaign commercials during election season!"

Here's the thing: I believe that the people complaining about negative ads *do* truly hate them. And being a voter living in what is often a swing state, I've been hammered with my fair share of negative ads over the airwaves. I'll agree—it's annoying.

That doesn't change the fact that *it works*.

This is the point I really want to drill for business owners: going negative *works*.

Again, it's not about pulling out a grenade launcher and blowing your competitor off the map. Going negative isn't about standing up and yelling that the other side sucks. It's about carefully using the power of comparison to create underdog status, engage with your audience, and ultimately craft an environment where your customer draws their own negative conclusions about your competitor, and chooses you, all by themselves.

Business leaders, and especially shareholders of large companies, are terrified to use this strategy for many reasons, not least of which is their constant and unrelenting terror of offending anyone in the slightest way. Businesses are so afraid to go negative at all that most of them don't even dip their toe in the water. They're afraid to take any kind of chance that a comparison drawn between them and their competitor—even if they're the ones controlling the comparison—might reflect poorly back on them.

Here's my question: are you in business to grow? Are you in business to gain market share and make money? Or are you in the business of being the same as every competitor in the marketplace? If it's the latter, continue to take the path of least resistance and "hope" you grow. Remember, you must be both relevant *and* unique to the customer— from *their* perspective, not yours.

Our culture of late is a feelings-driven, quick-to-offend nightmare landscape of customer opinion. Anything that can be construed as a direct attack from one company to another, or one candidate to another, spreads like wildfire on social media. It's no surprise that most businesses would rather avoid this key strategy, but you can avoid blowups entirely if you carefully and skillfully craft and target your negative campaign.

Refusing to go negative at all, though, is incredibly short-sighted. It's like a pilot who refuses to fly because the possibility exists that they'll screw up and crash the plane. Well, sure, that possibility exists, but here's a thought: *just don't screw up and crash the plane.* It's simple.

Direct attacks aren't always bad news for the attacking company, either. Like everything in the realm of negative advertising, it's all about skill.

T-Mobile recently pulled off a hell of a first strike at its biggest competitor, Verizon, with a single tweet. The CEO, John Legere, tweeted an article from *Business Insider* that showed that T-Mobile customers are more loyal than Verizon's, Sprint's, or AT&T's. He appended the article with the following line:

> *Probably because we treat them like actual people and not dollar signs! Looking at you, @Verizon...* 👀

My favorite part of this story is that he punctuated his tweet with the side-eye emoji, a move both hilariously humanizing and middle-finger sarcastic towards the target of his attack tweet. It's everything I've been saying—don't be a robot! Legere showed personality, humor, creativity, and above all else, strong leadership.

Also, notice how he only called out the biggest competitor, Verizon? He didn't mention Sprint or AT&T. There was no need—the press who picked up the story did all that work for him.

Most importantly, this wasn't an organic tweet from one CEO to another (i.e., a direct attack). This was a promoted tweet from T-Mobile's marketers. They realized, as the underdog, that the most powerful tool at their disposal was going on the attack. Their skill—the way they humanized the message, injected some humor, and kept it casual—is what made that tweet successful.

INTERVIEW: PETER KLEIN

Peter Klein might be most famously known as Gary Vaynerchuk's father-in-law, but more importantly, he's a former Corporate Officer of the Gillette Company and Nabisco Foods, responsible for Strategy, Planning, Business Development, and Global Marketing Services. He's also the co-author of *Think to Win: Unleashing the Power of Strategic Thinking*.

I recently interviewed him about the concept of going negative. Here's what he had to say:

> There are hard and soft reasons why companies don't do it—especially public companies. The board, and the key shareholders, don't want to see their brand in a negative way. In the 70s, 80s, and 90s, I remember tons of articles imploring companies not to go negative. They had headlines like, "The Negative Side of Negative Advertising."
>
> The mindset of these companies is that they can only be positive to communicate a positive branded position.
>
> But there may be middle ground—Bill Korn at Pepsi did the Coke vs. Pepsi taste test, and if anything, it elevated Pepsi big time. They felt they had a strong message on taste, especially with younger consumers, and felt they had a strategic imperative to pull the light and medium Coke drinkers into the Pepsi franchise. The result was incredibly strong, and it's what drove Coke to create New Coke, one of the biggest marketing disasters of all time within the consumer products' industry.

> Negative advertising sells big. It breaks through the clutter.
>
> The mindset that a positive brand has to run positive communication is old and outdated. You don't have to be doom and gloom, but you can and should go negative in a way that paints a comparison to your competition, and is positive for your product or service.

YOUR OFFENSE VERSUS THEIR DEFENSE

In the more than twenty years I've been in this business, I've learned that there's no worse place to be in a campaign than on the defensive.

This is not to say that we don't play defense on political campaigns; of course, we do. We have to. Our intent, however, is to be on offense *much* more than we're on defense. After all, when you're on offense, you have the ball. You can take it downfield for a touchdown. If you're on defense, the other team is the one with the ball, and you have to find a way to stop them, or create a turnover, before you can run it in for a touchdown. Offense is innovation.

When people, and especially business owners, are put on the defensive, they instinctively become paralyzed and reactive. They move too slowly, and when they finally do make a move, it's usually in the wrong direction. They're thinking emotionally; they're thinking with the primal part of their brain that tells them, *everyone is looking at you. Everyone thinks you're the bad guy.* Their sole focus becomes merely convincing customers that they're *not* the bad guy.

It reminds me of the five stages of grief. I call it the five reactive stages a business owner goes through with a negative ad:

1. First, they laugh at the ad made against them, and mock the other side for running it. *They're clowns. No one is going to take this seriously!*
2. Then they freeze; they realize people might be taking it seriously, and become paralyzed by fear.
3. Next, they fall into bureaucratic chaos. They flail around reactively: *We have to do something about this! Everybody think of something to do! Let's hold a bunch of meetings to come up with a plan!*
4. Acceptance. They realize that the comparison has taken hold in the customers' minds, and they've been left in the dust by their opponent.
5. Finally, they take action. They try to run a counter-attack ad, usually far too late to make a difference—or, it flops with a thud.

While they're busy working through the five stages, the business owners on offense are out gaining market share.

Business is a blood sport. Tony Robbins calls business owners "gladiators." Why would you hesitate to put everything you've got into your fight for market share?

By being creative and innovative, and crafting skilled messaging that plays on the psychology of not just your customers, but also your competitors, you can position yourself as the dominant force in your industry without actually owning the lion's share of the market. Pepsi did this; they were the underdog on the block looking to prove something, and they were hungry and willing to mix it up. Against Coke, they were David versus Goliath. And with the simplest ad concept that played on the human needs for social capital and acceptance, they managed to put Coca-Cola on the defensive to the extent that the bigger company backpedaled and blundered its way into destroying the very thing that had made it a juggernaut in the first place.

Also, consider what environment you're in—are you in a cutthroat industry? If your competition is using a "go negative" advertising strategy, and you aren't, you're running a major risk to your business. In politics, the day a candidate actually forbids their campaign team from engaging in negative ads is the day they lose. You have to play the game you're in if you want to win.

You can put your competitors on the ropes and gain market

share before they even realize they've lost it. By going negative, you can catch them off guard, and take advantage of their confusion, frustration, fear, and paralysis. You can go from the underdog to the top dog. Most importantly, by humanizing your brand with creative negative advertising, you can create priceless engagement with your customers and brand loyalty that money can't buy.

CHALLENGE YOURSELF: BE BOLD. BE SMART. TRY GOING NEGATIVE.

If you're still on the fence about going negative, try this exercise:

1. Identify your company's largest competitor in the market.

2. Using the "Challenge Yourself" brainstorming method from Chapter Five—pen and paper, with no electronic distractions, for thirty-five minutes— think of two ways your business is better than your competitor's, in the ways that matter most to your customers.

3. Get your team together and brainstorm ways you can draw comparisons based on the above results.

   If you're all-in on going negative, make it fun! Map out a large-scale, humorous attack wherein you publicly challenge your competitor on one key element that matters to your customers—a place where you shine, and where your competitor can't measure up. Create a press campaign for this challenge, and go BIG!

4. Bring in your marketing team and use research to align your thinking toward subtlety and creativity— and have them create ads that imply what your competitor is doing wrong by highlighting what you're doing right.

Bonus: How did this challenge work for you? Did you execute this in a smart way? If so, don't forget to check in with your fellow readers at http://facebook.com/ceophillipstutts. Remember, if you crush this challenge, I really want to hear about it—especially when I write the sequel to this book.

CHAPTER SEVEN

WHEN THE SH*%
HITS THE FAN

TACKLING THE INEVITABLE
CRISIS HEAD ON

"The road to bold is paved with failure, and this means that having a strategy in place to handle risk and learn from mistakes is critical."

PETER DIAMANDIS

With all the campaigns I've worked on, and having been behind the scenes in politics for decades, I'd thought I'd seen it all.

Let me assure you—the hacking of the Democratic National Committee during the 2016 presidential election was like *nothing* I've ever seen.

No one anticipated it. No one even came close to predicting that something like that could happen. In the days leading up to the Democratic National Convention in July 2016, when WikiLeaks published a trove of 20,000 emails hacked from the DNC server, everyone who worked in politics was just as knocked off their feet as everyone reading the news at home. It was a completely unprecedented crisis, and no one had any idea how to react.

I recently interviewed Donna Brazile, political strategist, Al Gore's 2000 campaign manager, author, former Chairwoman of the DNC, and author of *Hacks: The Inside Story of the Break-ins and Breakdowns That Put Donald Trump in the White House.* We talked primarily about crisis management, but she also gave me the following insight on the DNC hack.

> When we realized our emails, our donor base, and all our communication had been hacked, we were caught by surprise. That specific scenario wasn't something we had ever expected, or had prepared for. But we still had a plan in place to deal with an unforeseen crisis.
>
> We activated a crisis communications campaign. We didn't wait twenty-four hours to see what would leak; we had a plan prepared within a single hour. We needed to protect our infrastructure and ensure that

our product and assets wouldn't be compromised more than they already were.

We developed a strategy to respond to down-ballot candidates and races to make sure they weren't affected; our mindset was that it wasn't just us, but also our donors and candidates who would be impacted by the hack.

We were definitely caught off-guard, but thanks to our crisis preparation, we quickly had a proactive plan in place to address the issue of the hack ahead of the news cycle.

The DNC didn't invent this crisis plan after the crisis appeared; they had a strong, nimble, effective plan for how to deal with a crisis far ahead of shit actually hitting the fan. They had already asked themselves the question, *Okay, if a crisis hits, how do we deal with it?* They'd developed an action plan and knew exactly what needed to be done when the email hack was published.

Within a day of the leak's publication, they had a war room set up to handle all communication about the crisis. From that centralized unit, they were able to respond to any accusation, any negative comment on social media, any unflattering article. They were also able to counter-attack with positive stories and started to spin attention away from the hack and back on to their candidate's platform and campaign.

The most important thing they did? They didn't hide. They got out in front of the problem and addressed it head on.

So often, when faced with a crisis, people—and this goes for businesses, as well—stick their heads in the sand and pretend nothing is happening, hoping it will all go away if they just ignore the problem long enough.

People do this because they don't understand two key facts:

1. The faster you get accurate information out there, the more control you have over the way people react to your crisis.
2. Thanks to the rapid-fire immediacy of social media, the half-life of a crisis is relatively short—*as long as you don't ignore it*. If you do ignore it, the speed of social media escalation will all but ensure your destruction.

A great example of #2 can be found in just about everything President Trump does. When President Trump first took office, the media weren't accustomed to a president who so completely flouted the normal rules of engagement. Every new tweet, every new controversy, rolls right off his back, largely because the media doesn't really have time to obsess over it before he moves on to the next thing that outrages them all over again.

Recently, a reporter called me and asked about what must have been the five thousandth Trump crisis since he took office. She told me, "Everyone on Capitol Hill is saying this controversy spells the end of Trump."

I started laughing.

"What?" she demanded, incredulous.

"You know you guys are going to move on to the next thing in all of three hours," I said.

She refused to budge. "No. This is the biggest crisis yet. He can't come back from this one."

"Okay. Sure."

Guess what happened? Exactly nothing.

Social media is a double-edged sword when it comes to crisis management. On the one hand, if you play your cards right and get out in front of the crisis train, you can be assured that the speed of social media will blow that train past you within a small window of time.

The flip side is that if you do what so many people do, and try to ignore the problem until it goes away (it never does!), social media is like a giant echo chamber of outrage. The problem spins around and around in that echo chamber until it's ten times its size. Worse, you have *no* control over the way the problem is being perceived, because you're not part of the dialogue surrounding it. The fire spreads if you're not around to put it out.

When crisis hits—and it will hit everyone and every business, you need to face it immediately. The fastest way out is through.

THE THREE-STEP PLAN EVERY BUSINESS SHOULD HAVE PREPARED

It's not enough simply to rely on the speed and skill of your team to manage a crisis when it erupts; you need to have a plan of action in place. There will always be a crisis to deal with. It could be small, it could be huge—but it's inevitable. To make sure your business is well-primed to deal with it effectively, it's critical to constantly anticipate and plan for the unknown.

Donna Brazile and the DNC were able to handle a shit-hits-the-fan moment like no one had ever seen because they did the smart thing beforehand—they crafted a plan to follow if anything ever blew up in their faces. They stuck to process and made it through a summer and fall that presented constant unpredictable aftershocks to that first WikiLeaks data dump. The hits kept coming, but they stuck to their plan.

To run a business, lead a non-profit, or oversee a marketing program without a crisis communication infrastructure and action plan in place *before* crisis hits, is basically to ensure that your efforts will not enable you to weather the storm. And, in our current digital media environment, it's committing business suicide to leave crisis management preparation to chance.

There are three key political principles that any company should adopt as the foundation of their crisis management:

1. Have a team ready to spring into action and form a "war room" mentality the moment the crisis hits. Whether you are a business with 1,000 employees or ten, address any negative headline, blog post, or social media comment within a few hours. Get a plan. Get on top of it ASAP.
2. Shift your mindset toward honesty and transparency.

INTERVIEW: DONNA BRAZILE

Donna Brazile is an old friend of mine, and recently I interviewed her on the subject of crisis management.

These days, political campaigns market their candidates just like a brand. We launch campaigns in the same way, we message the same way, and we mirror what the branding experts do. We've adapted to the corporate environment.

Last year, with the hacking of the DNC, we responded not to protect ourselves, but to protect our brand. We activated a well-planned crisis communications campaign, and had counter-action out in the press within an hour.

Part of our strategy was also protecting down-ballot candidates—we had adapted well in advance to protect the entire organization, again like a brand instead of a single person.

No one anticipates a crisis. But they still happen, and when they do, you have to get ahead of the news cycle.

In our digital world, every inch of our digital infrastructure is under attack at all times. This includes our country, and it includes our business. Invest resources now in planning for the inevitable—prepare now, or pay for it later.

When you address a crisis, you must show empathy and assure the public you're going to make this better. *Honesty and openness is everything.*

3. The way you handle a crisis doesn't stop with the public side; people want to be reassured that a similar issue won't happen again. Resolve to figure out what caused the crisis internally, and be open—possibly publically—about how you plan to do better.

Should you stop with those three principles and call it a day?

Hell no.

Developing a plan for an "Oh, Shit!" crisis involves taking a long, hard look at your business and predicting where the cracks will show first when bad things happen.

You may be asking: what kind of event qualifies as a crisis? It could be a bad review on a social platform like Yelp, an accusation made by a customer or client, or a lawsuit that spills over into the public domain.

Whatever it is, create a solid series of steps you'll take to fix those cracks the second they appear. Play offense and don't take the chance that you and your people will respond quickly and correctly to right the ship; when crisis occurs, emotions run high. The best fallback is a clear communication and action plan that has already been tested and proven.

DO OPPOSITION RESEARCH—ON YOURSELF

If you have a proactive and well-tested plan in place to handle crises that hit your business, you're probably going to be able to get through them with minimal damage. However, ask yourself this question: do you know where your business is vulnerable?

As business owners, we're often completely focused on the ways our businesses are doing well, and how we can innovate and explore new ways to do even better. But have you ever taken the time to poke around and see what skeletons are hiding in your closet?

Here's something you should know: your competitors, or a disgruntled customer, will take that time, and they'll bring up anything they can to try to discredit you, especially in the age of social media. Worse, sometimes, they'll come at you anonymously—making it hard to fight back.

This happens in politics all the time, of course—every campaign has a team devoted to what we call *opposition research*. In fact, in one of the DNC data dumps WikiLeaks released in 2016, there was a treasure trove of opposition research on both Bernie Sanders and Donald Trump. This was used by the media to stoke outrage, but everyone who's ever worked in politics shrugged and said, "Yeah, and?"

Opposition research is a given in any political campaign, and no one working behind the scenes is surprised by it—in fact, they expect it. They expect it to the extent that any good campaign performs opposition research *on itself* to know exactly where they're going to get hit by their opponents, when the negative ads inevitably start flying.

If someone were to come in and conduct opposition research on your business right now, what would they find? Are all your taxes and payroll above reproach? Have you ever been sued?

Again—sticking your head in the sand *never works.*

I have a friend whose political marketing agency worked in a large state for a candidate who was running for governor. Trouble was, my friend's firm was being sued for defamation in the same state. The suit had lingered for over a year. It was completely frivolous and had no chance of finding for the plaintiff for several reasons, not least of which was that my colleague's firm was squarely protected under the First Amendment. However, none of that would have mattered to the opposition in the gubernatorial campaign, who simply could have splashed all over the media that their opponent's marketing firm was the subject of a defamation lawsuit.

Instead of keeping quiet about the suit, my friend went straight to the candidate and the campaign team and said, "Hey, look, I want to give you a heads up." She told the candidate's team the entire story, and was honest and open about where he stood with the lawsuit. She also made sure they understood that, if the lawsuit was brought up by the opposition, the campaign would need to have a plan in place to deal with it. The campaign was completely fine with the situation, and got to work right away on a crisis communication plan to execute should the vendor's lawsuit ever be used against them.

You have nothing to lose, and everything to gain, from knowing the potential pitfalls of your own company. Understand your strengths and weaknesses, and understand deeply every aspect of what's lurking in your closet.

HOW NOT TO HANDLE A CRISIS

This is an upsetting event to all of us here at United. I apologize for having to re-accommodate these customers. Our team is moving with a sense of urgency to work with the authorities and conduct our own detailed review of what happened. We are also reaching out to this passenger to talk directly to him and further address and resolve this situation.

It's almost breathtaking how bad a crisis-response that is for any business, let alone a Fortune 100 company.

The above statement, of course, was made by United Airlines' CEO Oscar Munoz in response to the incident on United Flight 3411 where a passenger was violently dragged off the overbooked flight in order to accommodate United employees who were needed at another airport. Ironically, just a month before, Oscar Munoz had been awarded "U.S. Communicator of the Year" by *PRWeek* magazine.

The incident on the plane had been filmed on another passenger's cell phone. The video of a seemingly confused older gentleman screaming as he was roughly pulled out of his seat and dragged down the aisle by his arms, bleeding, had gone viral. Within hours, it had incited the kind of outrage across the web that would be difficult for *any* company to come back from—let alone United, which already existed in the less-than-beloved airline industry.

What was United's response to the instant and fiery excoriation they were receiving across all social media platforms and every other corner of the web, not to mention round-the-clock news coverage of every digital and traditional media outlet?

The company was silent for nearly a full twenty-four hours, and then Oscar Munoz, U.S. Communicator of the Year, put out the utter gobbledygook you read above.

Twenty-four hours in the life of a crisis like this one might as well be twenty-four *years*. United had the opportunity to immediately respond with an unequivocal, emotional apology, but for some reason, they waited a day and let the fire on social media run out of control. And when they did release the tone-deaf mess above, they were *savaged* by pundits, PR pros, and the general public.

Munoz then circulated an internal memo that quickly went public. In it, he stated that the passenger in question had been "disruptive and belligerent," and that he stood by his employees. Once the news media and social networks got a hold of this memo, the fire turned into an inferno.

Munoz waited *another twenty-four hours* (are you sensing a trend?) before releasing a second statement:

The truly horrific event that occurred on this flight has elicited many responses from all of us: outrage, anger, disappointment. I share all of those sentiments, and one above all: my deepest apologies for what happened. ...I have committed to our customers and our employees that we are going to fix what's broken so this never happens again. We'll communicate the results of our review by April 30. I promise you we will do better.

This was closer to the mark, but it also rang false, because the entire world had already read the internal letter from Munoz that expressed the exact opposite sentiments. It was too little, too late.

By this point, the market value of United Airlines had plummeted $250 million.

Let's repeat this...the market value of United Airlines had plummeted $250 million!

The United crisis is a perfect example of tone-deafness in a culture where transparency and humanity are valued by the public above all else. In today's digital landscape, you simply *cannot* be tone deaf. You need to be aware of what your customers want to hear, and you need to show them that you hear their concerns and understand why they have them.

If you screw up, don't craft a generic, watered-down non-apology apology. Be open, be honest, and apologize like you would to your best friend, or your spouse. Show empathy, vulnerability, and the intent to fix your mistakes, to be better. It's the only way to earn back the trust of the public.

And please, for the love of God, don't ever start an apology with "If I offended anyone..." That non-apology is a surefire way to make you even *more* enemies!

Just recently, Equifax, one of the three major credit bureaus in the U.S., endured a massive data breach that saw as many as 143 million people's personal information hacked by cybercriminals. In an absolutely epic failure of crisis management, Equifax's former CEO Richard Smith, waited *three weeks* to tell the board of directors about the hack. He found out about the data breach on July 31, 2017, and spent the next twenty days hiring legal and investigative experts instead of informing the company and the public of the impending firestorm. He has since retired with a $90 million golden parachute.

Ridiculous!

Apologize. Take responsibility. Be open, be empathetic, be real.

Most importantly: *act fast.*

GET IN THE GAME

When things go wrong, a company has to tell its story. A company has to have a plan in place to share how it's addressing the public's concerns. It has to show how it will be proactive and fix the problem.

Here's the interesting thing: being proactive when it comes to dealing with a crisis is actually contrary to human instinct. We all have the impulse to duck and cover when it comes to bad news—"Nothing to see here, move along!" No one wants their lives disrupted. Even I did this, back when I was originally diagnosed with my incurable esophageal disease—I stuck my head in the sand and pretended nothing was happening.

In all the years I've been working as a marketer, 99 percent of my clients have reacted with the head-in-the-sand instinct. "Let's just stay quiet and let it go away on its own," they'll tell me. Or, God forbid, "How can we cover this up?" That's the kind of client that represents a crisis to *my* business, and my rapid response is to drop them as quickly as possible.

You'd be hard-pressed to find a business owner, though, who is enthusiastic about getting out in front of a problem and dealing with it head on. At the end of the day, it's tough to admit when you've screwed up, especially if few have noticed your screw-up yet. The problem in hiding, though, is of course that *it will be noticed eventually.*

Take the story I told earlier about George W. Bush's DUI. The campaign was totally blindsided by this, but that doesn't mean that once it knew, they were surprised that the news had come out. *Of course* a hidden DUI, for a guy running for the most public office in the world, would have come out eventually. Had his senior lieutenants known about it from the start, they would have advised him to put it front and center right away. And frankly, the voters would quickly have moved on from the story.

Our society craves humanized leadership. Had Bush made a statement about the DUI at the beginning of the campaign, honest and from the heart, we might not have seen such a razor-thin margin that led to the Florida recount.

All it would have taken was openness, transparency, and vulnerability: "In 1977, I had a DUI in Maine. It's something I'm terribly embarrassed about, but Laura and I think it's important to talk about it openly, because driving under the influence kills. I regret it more than anything I've ever done. It was inexcusable. We've talked to our children about drunk driving, and we encourage you to talk to yours. We should learn from our mistakes. I certainly have. Everyone has the potential to make a life-altering mistake they can't take back. I'm grateful I was given a second chance."

The public would have loved this. It shows honesty, character, and humanity. It shows *leadership*.

In 2000, George W. Bush lost the state of New Mexico by 366 votes, out of 573,200 votes cast. He also lost the national popular vote. In order to win the Electoral College, and thus the presidency, we had to turn Florida into a battleground. There's no doubt in my mind that if he had gotten out in front of the DUI problem from the outset, I would never have found out what a hanging chad is, and we all could have gone to bed Election Night 2000 secure in our win.

Business owners, just like many politicians, will always be receptive to someone who validates their instinct. They think they're being proactive if, after a crisis hits, they hire an outside marketing or PR firm to come in and help them salvage their reputation. (Trust me, I know—my firm gets hired in these moments all the time.) That's being *reactive*, not proactive. Worse, many times after a business owner hires an outside firm to help in such a crisis, they're forced to put trust and control in the hands of others—not because they want to, but because they have to. Those PR or marketing firms usually just want the paycheck, and will often simply validate the business owner's instinct to either hide completely, or put out a generic watered-down statement first and *then* hide. It's the blind leading the blind. In politics, we call it the walk of death.

Back in 2009, when the Deepwater Horizon rig owned by BP exploded and oil started gushing into the Gulf of Mexico, the reaction of the company was slow and clumsy. Gaffe after gaffe in the aftermath of the spill kept London-based BP in the headlines. They were raked over the coals. Their market share plummeted. They had an internal crisis communications plan in place for damage control in a crisis, but for some reason, they ignored most of it.

Their CEO, Tony Hayward, at one point complained, "I'd like my life back."

Definitely not the best response to a situation that had cost eleven lives and countless jobs along the Gulf Coast. At the time, I was working for a client with direct access to a governor who was fielding the drastic needs of thousands of people impacted by the oil spill all along the coast of his state. Tony Hayward wanted his life back? Get in line—the back of it!

When you've cost people their livelihoods, and they don't know where their next paycheck is coming from, the best response is to immediately take charge and fix the problem—but more importantly, to show a little humanity. With BP, they should have exhibited a sensitivity to the fact that there were eleven families grieving their loved ones. Talk to the families to ask what they need and how they can help. Put the wheels in motion to support the fishermen and small business owners who will likely never recover from the catastrophe of the oil spill. Get out in front of the problem. *Be proactive.*

The settlement eventually agreed to by BP cost $20 billion. If they had handled the situation more effectively, I'm convinced it would have been a tenth of that amount.

One of the hardest things for a business owner to do is proactively address something that hasn't occurred yet—or that has occurred, but that they hope will go away. They drag their feet in responding. They try to shirk blame or responsibility.

In politics, this would mean the end of a candidacy or a career. This is not to say there aren't politicians who stick their heads in the sand in response to crisis; I definitely see it all the time. In the long run, most are not successful or they don't last long in public life. Personally, I can't imagine being entrusted with the marketing of a political campaign, and having an avoidance mentality. "Well, our candidate said something dumb on the campaign trail again...but maybe no one heard him. Maybe the press didn't notice. Maybe our opponent won't run a dozen negative ads hammering on this dumb quote. I sure hope we don't have to deal with this issue."

If that sounds absurd, it's because *it is absurd.* No political campaign could possibly survive for long with that mentality.

The *only* mentality that works in politics is action. When confronted with a crisis, smart political teams get in the game and get to work. They begin to execute their prepared crisis management plan immediately.

The *smartest* political teams take it a step further; they don't just get in the game, they get *ahead* of the game. They do their opposition research on themselves, discover everything that can be used against them, and then put all of it out there for public view—because it's definitely going to come out at some point, and by releasing it themselves, at least they have some control of the narrative.

As a business owner, you're probably not going to face a crisis the size of BP, Equifax, or United Airlines. Your crisis might be as small scale as three bad Yelp reviews in a row. It doesn't matter that this is of a magnitude smaller than lost lives and damaged livelihoods; it's significant to your business, and it can't be ignored. If you have a plan in place ahead of time, you have a roadmap out of the crisis, and you're more likely to come through as unscathed as possible.

What this comes down to is control. Your story as a business is going to be written no matter what you do. Would you rather that you write it? Or, would you rather that it was written by someone else—public opinion, the media, your competitors?

Take control. Own your story.

CHALLENGE YOURSELF
(IF SHIT HITS THE FAN)

Answer these two questions:

If a crisis hit your business this afternoon, 1) what do you think it would most likely be, and 2) how would you handle it?

If your answer isn't clear and you don't have a planned series of steps that gets out in front of the problem and shows humanized, empathetic leadership, you've got a problem.

If you're drawing a blank, consider these steps:

1. Come up with one crisis that could potentially occur for your business in the next twelve to twenty-four months—anything from a bad Yelp review to a public lawsuit.

2. Create a crisis action outline or a plan with your team.

3. If you can't think of a potential crisis for your business, use a real-world crisis that sank one of your competitors, and complete step two.

Bonus: How did this challenge work for you? Most readers won't share their real-world crisis story, so how about this: if you see a crisis story in the news and notice their execution flaws, missteps in handling, or if they actually did the right thing and took back control of their story, share it here: http://facebook.com/ceophillipstutts.

CHAPTER EIGHT

YOU WILL FAIL

DON'T QUIT, BE SMARTER

"Everyone fails. Highly successful people fail many more times than the rest of the world, and with much higher stakes at hand."

LEWIS HOWES

If you're hoping to accomplish anything of substance in this world, you will experience failure. It's unavoidable, and it's a good thing.

As Tim Ferriss states so well, "failure is feedback." It's feedback from the world telling you where you need to adjust, pivot, and improve. A lot of people in our society have lost sight of that. They expect life to give them a trophy for participating, and they see failure as a signal from the universe that it just "wasn't meant to be."

If you have that mindset about failure, you will rarely succeed. Virtually every politician to hold a major office has lost a race at some point in their career. Every successful business owner has missed their goals somewhere along the way. The difference between those with massive success and those that don't is simple: the success stories listened to the lessons in their failures. They reflected, adapted, and got back in the game.

The people who never succeeded? They gave up early.

To most business owners and non-profit heads, the key pain point of today's business landscape is digital marketing. They hear from all directions that digital marketing is the key to success, that it can transform their organization and 10x their success, but when they attempt to execute it, they're lost. It's a mystery to them. They try tactics they read or hear about from other business leaders, but they fail because they have no idea how to target digital marketing to their unique organization. This failure brings with it frustration and anxiety—business owners can sense that the market is shifting, and that they need to make digital marketing work for them, but every time they try, they fail. It's demoralizing, and it triggers the paralysis of fear.

Of the hundreds of business owners and CEOs I've spoken

to about digital marketing, every single one has a story of failure and frustration when it comes to digital marketing.

But does that mean they should give up?

Definitely not. They just need to be pointed in the right direction, and given the tools and knowledge to take off.

Failure enables innovation. For a great example of this, look no further than former President Bill Clinton. In 1974, Clinton, at the time a twenty-eight-year-old law professor, ran for the House of Representatives in Arkansas. Clinton was counting on the anti-establishment sentiments permeating the country after the Watergate scandal, and while he did make the race incredibly close, he lost to Republican incumbent John Paul Hammerschmidt by 4 percent of the vote.

Dealt the first real failure of his career, Clinton did what all successful people do. He reflected, adapted, innovated, and recommitted himself to the fight.

Clinton realized that at twenty-eight, he simply didn't have the pedigree to carry such a public office in Arkansas. So, in 1976, Clinton ran for a position where he'd face almost no competition, the Arkansas Attorney General. Winning the race easily, he spent two years building up his public profile, until 1978, when he successfully ran for Governor of Arkansas.

He was the youngest elected governor in the history of the United States. Four years previously, he was a failed political upstart teaching law at a university.

However, as we all know, Clinton's history has told us that he was far from done failing. Two years after becoming the youngest governor in history, Clinton would lose reelection, becoming the youngest ex-governor in history.

There's debate over what caused him to lose popularity in that time frame. Some point to unpopular laws, others to PR crises, while others believe he did a poor job of fostering a strong public image. Regardless of which factors combined to tank his approval rating, the lesson in this failure for Clinton was clear: Never get complacent. Never believe the race is over, because it never is.

By 1982, Clinton was back on the ballot. He won his election, retook the governor's office, and learning from those two previous failures, he went on to hold that office for ten consecutive years. He would then go on to be a two-term United States President.

None of these victories would have been possible had he

not failed. He would have never been nominated for president—let alone won the presidential election—without first failing spectacularly.

This ability to fail, and fail well, is a trait Clinton shares with all victors in both the political and business spheres.

THE BEST POLITICIANS FAIL

What does every U.S. president from Jimmy Carter to Barack Obama have in common?

They all lost a major election prior to being elected president.

Starting from the back, Jimmy Carter ran for governor in 1966. He didn't even make it through the Democratic primary, finishing in third. Carter had run what many considered a naïve campaign. He claimed he was "too complicated" to really be nailed down by a single party, he used barely any modern election tactics in terms of advertising or analytics, and he did a terrible job of fundraising.

As a result, he was left embarrassed and deeply in debt after losing the 1966 election. He spent the next four years reflecting, adapting, and recommitting himself to the fight. In 1970, he ran a much more mature campaign, using what was then considered cutting-edge analytics and professional advertising, and tied himself more closely to the conservative platform of southern voters.

As a result, he won the 1970 election for Governor of Georgia, and would go on to win the presidency in 1976.

Ronald Reagan, the president who succeeded Jimmy Carter, was even more of a serial failure. A former actor who didn't run his first race until he was fifty-four, Reagan was crushed as the third-place Republican presidential candidate in 1968.

Reagan then won two terms as Governor of California. He reflected on his loss, adapted his strategy, and recommitted to the fight. In 1976, he ran for president again, and was again defeated in the Republican primary—only this time, he lost by an extremely narrow margin.

Reagan again took the loss in stride, learning from his repeated failures. In 1980, Reagan launched his third presidential campaign, this time winning against incumbent Jimmy Carter.

This pattern carries on throughout presidential history:

- George H. W. Bush lost a U.S. Senate race in 1964

and the 1980 Republican presidential nomination (to Ronald Reagan).

- George W. Bush lost an election for U.S. Congress in 1978, then didn't run for office again until 1994, when he won the race for Governor of Texas. Six years later, he won the presidency.
- Barack Obama won his first election for a seat in the Illinois state senate in 1996 but then lost a U.S. Congressional primary race in 2000 by 30 percentage points (a blowout!). This was just eight years before being elected as the first African-American President in U.S. history.
- Even Donald Trump dipped his toe in the presidential waters for a brief period in 2000 (as the Reform Party candidate), before withdrawing from the race after garnering little support.

It's not just presidential candidates who tend to lose elections before winning them. Some of the most inspiring politicians I've ever worked with had to learn lessons from failure before they could finally succeed.

The example that springs to mind is Bobby Jindal. Bobby is one of the most inspiring people you'll ever meet. He has a sort of "governing gene," a natural inclination for leadership and governance the likes of which I've hardly ever seen.

INTERVIEW: PETE HEGSETH

Pete Hegseth, FOX News Senior Political Analyst, military officer, and former U.S. Senate candidate, recently sat down with me to talk about failure.

I was the senior counter-insurgency instructor in Afghanistan when I was deployed there. It was tough terrain. Later, when I ran for office, I didn't properly read the terrain, and I lost. I'm not afraid to fail, and every failure brings a new opportunity.

I ran for office in a long shot, and I lost. But during that campaign, I established relationships and opportunities that were invaluable to me in moving toward success. I solicited feedback from these trusted relationships, and leveraged that feedback to greater success.

Once I'd had some small success, I leveraged that into much greater wins. I grew my brand and became a national media personality.

I've seen a lot of entrepreneurial efforts fail, and it's because most business owners refuse to take any risks at all, even a small one. Businesses invest so much of their money on the back end that they get scared and build an 80 percent solution.

Frankly, taking a huge risk—running for political office—and failing was what leveraged my business into success.

But in 2003, during his first campaign for governor of Louisiana, he was only thirty-one years old. His pedigree for someone his age was impressive, but he'd never been in that sort of campaign before. Unprepared for the racist attack ads his opponent would run in the election, Bobby wound up losing the popular vote by just a few percentage points.

However, he learned quickly from his failure, and immediately began running a new campaign, this time for a congressional seat in the House of Representatives. Freshly educated by his failure in 2003, Bobby Jindal was elected in 2004 as the second Indian-American in the history of the U.S. Congress.

To put this in perspective, Bobby Jindal won a congressional seat in a district where David Duke—the famous white supremacist—previously came within a hair of winning the seat only five years before. It takes generational talent and character to cause such a major swing in votes.

Bobby was serving Louisiana when Hurricane Katrina struck in 2005, and quickly showed the nation how powerful a leader he was. He was phenomenal at managing the crisis from an operational perspective, and he made sure to maintain a real presence for his constituents, going into hospitals after the storm, working to help people rebuild homes, and openly criticizing the poor preparedness of the state for such a storm.

His popularity surged, and he was elected governor—the same position he had earlier failed to secure—in 2007. He was then reelected in a landslide in 2011.

In all of these examples, we're talking about leaders who rose to incredible political heights, where they were entrusted with responsibility over millions of Americans. Every single one of them failed before they reached the top of the mountain.

This lesson is perhaps most dramatic in politics, where every race has a clear winner and loser, but it's no different in business.

IT'S NOT JUST THE POLITICIANS

When we talk about CEOs who have "won" over the past few decades, Steve Jobs is first and foremost in everyone's mind.

The man is credited with some of the earliest innovations in modern computers, innovations upon which he built some of the most iconic companies in history. In 1976, Steve Jobs, Steve Wozniak, and Ronald Wayne launched Apple Computer. Nine years later, when Apple had grown from a small project housed in Steve Jobs's garage to a multimillion- dollar corporation, Jobs was in the midst of a power struggle at Apple, leading him to resign in 1985.

He built one of the most important companies in the world, and promptly lost it.

Learning from his failure, Jobs spent the next several years innovating in smaller businesses like NeXT and Pixar. Apple, meanwhile, stayed stagnant. In 1997, Jobs returned to Apple to reclaim his position as CEO, and his constant innovating led the company to its current stratospheric position on the world business stage.

Without the lessons he learned in his initial failure, Jobs would not have been able to lead his companies to the successes they achieved. Had he quit after that initial failure, none of those companies would have changed the world in the ways that they did.

To succeed, you have to be prepared to fail. All the time, I see business owners who are mystified by digital marketing, who keep trying to make it work but fail over and over again, and who just want to give up and pay a digital marketing agency to do the work for them.

Let me be blunt: handing over the keys to your business's success *is* failure.

It's not about quitting or washing your hands of the problem. Those who will thrive in the upcoming economic and market shifts are those who, when faced with failure, will get smarter, adapt, and innovate to win. And failing at the outset is what *motivates* that adaptation.

You have to embrace failure—you can't accept a participation trophy. In politics, like in business, if you don't feel failure, you will never learn the lessons necessary for true success.

I had to learn this, and re-learn this, in my own business.

HOW FAILURE LEVELED UP MY COMPANY

One of the lessons of failure is that it never ends. Presidents lose reelection, and even the ones who serve two terms always lose at least one legislative battle. There is always an area in which you can improve, and nothing will instruct you in your weaknesses the way failure will.

I learned this firsthand with my company.

When I first started my political digital marketing agency,

I brought with me the lessons I'd learned in the trenches of the political campaign world. Because of those learnings, I was able to quickly out-compete my competitors.

When I began handling marketing for businesses through my firm, I used political lessons to win for my clients. I was walking into situations where owners had been so burned by digital marketers that they were convinced the whole industry was fraudulent. The only reason they'd meet with me was because they needed new business, and I promised that I would do things completely different than the marketers in the business world. I would communicate every stage of the plan early—the exact ROI we were aiming for, how we were going to measure it, and if we were on target at every stage.

The same way that Ronald Reagan's motto of "Trust but verify" resonated with so many voters, this transparency and willingness to adapt to their needs resonated with all of my early clients. If my clients weren't seeing the ROI of our digital marketing plan, I didn't say, "Well, we have you in a twelve-month contract, so we're going to wait and see if things change." (Secret #1!) I immediately dove in to figure out how we could get things back on track. Why? Because we have to win in politics in order to be successful. Why wouldn't any digital agency have that exact mindset for marketing businesses?

I launched my political digital marketing company in 2015, and we grew it 500 percent very quickly, scaling up to more than twenty full-time employees. A lot of this success was due to the lessons I'd learned through failures in politics.

Unfortunately, though, I had more failing to do before I could reach the next level.

When we started expanding, I felt it was important that I have a large role in the hiring process. The only problem was this: I'm terrible at hiring.

I'm good at taking an idea, getting incredibly excited about it, and putting in whatever it takes to make it successful. That's a trait anyone whose succeeded in politics has—unrelenting energy and optimism.

However, that very trait can make it difficult to take an eight-figure business and triple it.

Hiring is a great example of this. In order to successfully campaign for an individual, you have to be a natural champion of others. You have to get excited about a person's potential.

I get incredibly excited and passionate about running

my business, coming up with amazing ideas for clients, and watching my team execute. I bring this passion to job interviews, and this was the source of my problem. Without realizing it, I was selecting people who matched my passion and excitement—people who *wanted* to come work for the firm, but who weren't the best skill fit. I'd let my enthusiasm and how much I liked their passion cloud my instincts, which were telling me that these people were all wrong for their roles.

Those people didn't last long at our company, but their exit was damaging to our culture. I realized I needed to fire myself from the hiring process. So, that's exactly what I did.

I hired a couple of experts to run the hiring process, and I removed myself from it completely. I don't get involved in any of the interviews or assessments—of which there are many! We now do personality assessments, culture assessments, and several other tests to make sure the person is the right fit both for their role and for our culture.

We went from a hiring success rate of around 40 percent (60 percent failure!) to a success rate of around 95 percent in just a year. It was the catalyst for the company doubling in size and revenue.

If I hadn't been able to see the hiring problem as my own

failure, and instead blamed the marketing talent pool, the economy, my clients, or the validity of our model, my company would have stagnated forever at that same level.

In any industry, the biggest successes are the ones who failed early and adapted. This goes deeper than just politics and small business. Even in the media world, the most popular shows weren't always huge successes.

The path to success is nearly always through failure and iteration. And when it comes to the digital marketing of your business, if you can't adapt—or if your marketers can't adapt—you are doomed to stay right where you are... or worse.

STAY ON TOP OF THE CHANGING TIDE

Nobody likes to fail. It's a terrible feeling, and when you're the leader of a business or a non-profit, you have other people depending on you, so your failure is amplified even more.

I understand completely what that feels like. And, based on the conversations I've had with CEOs and business owners, the digital marketing space has created a wave of failure and frustration that makes it difficult to want to keep going. I understand completely the instinct to simply hand off digital marketing to an outside expert, and focus on the things you feel you can crush, rather than the thing that's crushing you.

But here's what you have to remember: failure is inherent to business. It's *definitely* going to happen at some point. Handing it over to someone who is incentivized to do the bare minimum only compounds that failure—whereas you can actually *overcome* it, if you think outside the box.

If we're going to talk about bouncing back from failure, there's one company that makes a particularly good case study, and that's Uber.

Look, nobody can claim that Uber had a great 2017, or even a great 2016, for that matter. On paper, Uber is a world-class company, heading for an IPO in the future and changing the face of personal transportation. The headlines, though, tell a different story.

Following defeat in gaining market dominance in China in 2016, 2017 saw the company fielding scandal after scandal. Uber was in the news constantly for its workplace culture of rampant sexual harassment; the exit of its President, Jeff Jones; the exposure of secret initiatives to get around government regulators; fraud lawsuits from its own investors; and potential intellectual property theft, which led to a massive legal battle with Google. In the thick of all of this controversy, Uber's embattled CEO, Travis Kalanick, resigned.

The case study here is not Kalanick's difficult 2017, but rather the way the former CEO started the company.

Travis Kalanick didn't just come up with a nifty idea and launch a product; he created a movement. When Uber first launched in select cities, it wasn't just a ride you could call; it was a way to be a part of the future, part of the changing tide. Customers wanted to be part of something bigger than themselves.

Does this sound familiar?

Kalanick essentially treated the launch and growth of Uber as a political campaign, with Uber as the candidate, and it worked brilliantly. In order to launch in certain cities, he had to get political; the constant threat and squeeze of government regulations threatened Uber's expansion. Kalanick found himself, as the CEO of one of the fastest-rising startups in the world, visiting city councils and passionately persuading disgruntled regulators to allow Uber to operate. By the end of 2013, Uber's legal costs were $1 million per year, but by the end of 2014, Uber scored a valuation of $40 billion, and Kalanick himself was estimated to have a net worth of $3 billion.[1]

Every time a roadblock appeared in front of Kalanick, he pivoted and innovated. When the company began experiencing huge pressure from regulators, it invested heavily in self-driving cars. When Uber had to admit defeat in China, it pivoted to double down on UberEATS and further expansion to other countries. This volatility meant that Uber has had to deal with several PR nightmares, but the company is currently one of the highest-valued companies in the world, a unicorn with endless opportunities for expansion.

Travis Kalanick may be on the bottom now, but don't count him out. He thinks with a political mindset and knows that failure is one of the most powerful motivators that exists.

You will fail—especially when it comes to digital marketing implementation. There's no way around it. You will make mistakes, and your business will suffer. You don't have to let that be the end of the story, though.

Get up off the mat and innovate. Success is born out of being on the bottom and wanting nothing more than to claw your way to the top.

1   Petroff, Alanna. *The Rise and Fall of Uber CEO Travis Kalanick. CNN Money*. June 21, 2017. http://money.cnn.com/2017/06/21/technology/uber-ceo-travis-kalanick-timeline/index.html.

CHALLENGE YOURSELF: THE GROWTH MINDSET

1. Commit to understanding the game of digital marketing so that failure doesn't paralyze your growth mindset.

2. Sit down with your marketing team and brainstorm *small* ideas for digital marketing growth, aimed at overcoming a current obstacle or area of limited growth. The key is that the ideas are small—test-worthy and fail-worthy—and it won't cost you a lot of money to try them.

3. Once you've got them down, have your marketing firm implement them. If they don't work, ask yourself: *what did we learn, and how can we grow as a result?* If one of those ideas does work, though, it could be a huge new add-on or vertical for your business.

Bonus: How did this challenge work for you? How have you used failure to grow even bigger? Do you think your story can help other business owners? If so, check in with your fellow readers at http://facebook.com/ceophillipstutts.

CHAPTER NINE

DISRUPTION IS COMING

ADAPT, BE PROACTIVE OR DIE

"The quality of your life is in direct proportion to the amount of uncertainty you can comfortably deal with."

TONY ROBBINS

Certainty is one of the greatest traps we face as humans. We can't help ourselves; we crave it. We want to know for sure what's going to happen next, whether it's in business, politics, or just life in general.

Politicians often want to be certain that a certain action will have a certain result. "If I come out in opposition to this bill, I will be more popular with my constituents."

In life, we feel the same way. "If I marry this person, I'll be happy forever." When we feel uncertain, we scare ourselves into inaction.

In business, like in politics and life, inaction is a killer. Owners often want certainty and a guarantee on their digital marketing campaign spend. They want to know that if they spend $250,000, they'll see $1,000,000 in returns.

They hold back from taking action until a marketing agency comes along and promises them an easy, fail-proof strategy to get their outcome. The agency's promise is invariably a lie, because there *is* no easy, no-fail strategy with a guaranteed ROI in today's business world—marketing is by its very nature extremely difficult. Now, with digital marketing bifurcating the landscape, it's challenging, confusing and leaving business owners uncertain of the future. It also holds the keys to explosive business growth if planned and executed correctly.

The digital marketing world has been disrupted, and is continually being disrupted—meaning that whatever your strategy is, your business will need to proactively adapt with the technology, platforms, and eyeballs it needs in order to stay on top. In today's world, there is no easy route; the uncertainty has hit a height we've never seen before.

Waiting on a digital marketing plan that will succeed 100 percent of the time, doing the same thing you've always done in the past, is a losing game.

Volatility is not an aberration. Volatility is the rule. The future is uncertain; it will change and evolve in drastic ways, but if you are not pushing your chips in and making informed, proactive choices, then you are embracing paralysis and guaranteeing that you will not succeed.

PROACTIVE POLITICS = WINNING

When Hurricane Katrina hit in the summer of 2005, George W. Bush took a lot of flak for flying over New Orleans aboard Air Force One to observe the disaster. He didn't initially get out in front of the storm, didn't have a real strategy in place, and instead just reacted to what happened. The poor optics around this tragedy would plague him for the rest of his term as president.

You see this all the time in politics. The politicians who are proactive in crisis meet a level of certainty their voter is looking for—and they are the ones who win, even though a politician's future is always uncertain due to the ever-looming Election Day.

Political marketers have to be able to handle the extreme volatility and take calculated, proactive risks to succeed.

To understand the volatility political marketers are dealing with, you have to understand how quickly politicians' trajectories can change. All the time, they deal with clients who plan to run for one office, deciding they don't want to run for anything, and then changing their mind at the last minute to run for a completely different office.

For example, one of my clients was once planning a run for their state's governor. My company was counting on him being one of our biggest clients that year, and we were gearing up for a massive campaign.

At the last second, we received word that the president was going to nominate them for a high-level position. A nomination meant that they would no longer be running for governor, meaning we would no longer be running their campaign—in a roundabout way, the president had stolen our biggest client of the year.

But then, as so often happens in politics, a PR crisis struck. Suddenly, the president wasn't so sure of the nomination, and ultimately decided to drop our client as a nominee. *Boom*—we were instantly back in business. Or so we thought...

We talked to the client, got reenergized for the campaign, and began putting together our strategies and assets. Then, one day, our candidate randomly called and told us that he was so frustrated with politics over the lost nomination, he'd lost interest in running for any office at all.

For the second time, we'd lost our biggest client of the year.

Then (yes—the saga continues!), by some stroke of luck, one of the sitting senators from his state announced they would retire, and the vacancy piqued his interest. Suddenly, we had our client back, albeit for a very different but very big race.

You'd think the drama would have ended there, right? Stay in your seat.

Shortly after deciding to run for the Senate, he changed his mind again. He discovered that a local congressperson was going to run for the empty Senate seat, leaving their congressional seat empty. He decided that he actually wanted to run for the open congressional seat, not the U.S. Senate seat he originally was interested in. *Finally*, settled on a race, we were able to pursue a winning strategy.

As a business, how could we possibly have planned for that? Here's something you may not know: that's actually *not* an atypical journey for a political client to take. Campaign decisions tend to twist and turn. As a marketer who serves politicians, I have to build a company full of people who can deal with that insane level of uncertainty and volatility.

It has prepared me unbelievably well as the global economy undergoes disruption at a scope and scale that has never been seen before.

For years, the model of political marketing was reactive and flawed. It worked like this: political marketing agencies hired top talent during election years. Then, immediately following the election, they would let everyone go. They had no clients left, so they got rid of their employees. The agencies would go lean for ten months until the next round of elections, and then they'd ramp up hiring again.

This was reactive, and it made it very hard to retain the top talent that would ultimately prepare us to help our clients win.

We use a different, proactive strategy at my political marketing agency. In 2016, instead of paying myself the profits from successful campaigns, I reinvested that money into hiring the best talent as soon as the election season was over, when all the best talent were free agents. We went from seven employees to twenty—nearly tripling our size—in an off-election year. That simply doesn't happen in the political marketing world.

However, we operate from a place of confidence, not fear. We know that the future will be volatile, that politicians will change their minds, that upstart candidates will emerge out of nowhere, and that the surest bets in the world will be derailed by unforeseen forces.

We can't control that, but we can be proactive. We can hire the very best talent, and be confident that as circumstances change at breakneck speed, we will always have the best team to handle them, and therefore be positioned to win.

As it turns out, this basic principle is not so different in business.

BUSINESSES THAT HIDE FROM VOLATILITY LOSE

The world is changing. The majority of jobs that we think of as traditional or stable may be gone in the not-so-distant future. Technology will change, culture will change, our basic outlook of the world will change, and all of these changes will have consequences.

The natural inclination for business owners is to think, "Well, that change doesn't immediately affect my business, so I don't need to adapt."

But what about the ripple effect?

I already gave the example earlier of the ripple effect of self-driving cars. You can apply the same principle to just about any industry. For instance, when we're able to 3D-print meat, what happens to agriculture? What happens to the restaurant industry? What happens to grocery stores? How does it change health regulations? Will the reduction in livestock reduce carbon dioxide emissions? What effect will that have on our governmental policy and infrastructure?

Cars and agriculture are just two innovations, but their effects will ripple like an earthquake in the not so distant future. Now imagine hundreds, or thousands, of innovations occurring in quick succession, and you now have an accurate forecast of what's to come.

Business owners that want to put up blinders and keep trudging forward, only reacting when the change is beating down their business, are destined to fail. Like old-school political marketing agencies, their fear of uncertainty will destroy them.

When those businesses work with marketers who have a similar fear, whose strategies are purely reactive, the issue is only compounded.

The companies that are willing to prepare and execute in the face of uncertainty are the ones that will win.

This isn't a prediction based on my confidence in Silicon Valley's ability to innovate at rapid speed. This is a cycle we've seen throughout modern history. Peter Diamandis once gave a speech on this topic, wherein he showed a picture of New York City in 1903. The city is full of horses and buggies. He shows another similar picture of New York City in 1913, and it's completely different. There's one horse and buggy in sight—everything else on the road is an automobile.

With the rapid transition to cars, everything changed. New industries formed, old industries died, and the way people moved around the world fundamentally changed. The ripple effect of this shift touched nearly everyone in America, and it happened in just ten years.

Another obvious example of a company that capitalized on volatile markets by proactively innovating is Amazon. Jeff Bezos launched Amazon with the lofty goal to become a fundamental part of all commercial transactions—which was especially bold when you consider that Amazon originally was just a tiny, single, HTML-page online book retailer.

Amazon launched in the mid-90s, at a time when dot-com companies were popping up at a rapid clip, but even then Amazon was different. Whereas other tech companies were launching in reaction to the newfound attention and investments in the space, Amazon was always playing a much longer, proactive game.

As Jeff Bezos said:

> "The long-term approach is rare enough that it means you're not competing against very many companies because most companies want to see a return on investment in, you know, one, two, three years... I'm willing for it to be five, six, seven years. So just that change in timeline can be a very big competitive advantage."

Amazon was betting that by creating a customer-centric, fully transparent marketplace, they could disrupt physical retail entirely. With such lofty ambitions, Amazon grew slowly by investor standards, only reaching profitability in 2001. It did something, however, that most of its contemporary tech companies couldn't do—Amazon survived the tech bubble of 2000.

Most of the companies that failed when the tech bubble burst were built as a reaction to the sudden confidence in the tech industry. When that confidence went away, so did those companies.

Because Amazon was proactively innovating, they were able to survive the immense instability of that time period, and that dynamic of always staying one step ahead has remained Amazon's calling card.

For example, as web apps became more popular and sites became more robust, more and more transactions became purely digital. People weren't just buying physical goods from the internet; they were buying digital goods as well. Amazon, of course, was ahead of this trend, launching Amazon Web Services, a suite of hosting services commonly referred to as "the backbone of the internet." AWS is considered one of the most profitable products ever.

Similarly, as automation threatens to disrupt shipping, Amazon is already ahead of the game. Jeff Bezos announced in 2013 that Amazon was working on drones that could guarantee same-day delivery for customers.

Obviously, not every company can be Amazon, but every business owner can learn from Bezos's lesson of leaning in to volatility and making proactive moves to stay ahead.

IT'S NOT JUST ABOUT TECHNOLOGY

When we talk about innovation and disruption, we immediately think of the tech world, but a business can be innovative without building a new app.

A great example of this is Peter Mallouk's investment firm, Creative Planning.

In 2004, Peter was managing roughly $100 million, which is a decent amount, but not an incredible amount of money in that industry. Looking around at his business, he had a realization.

Peter realized that stockbrokers are incentivized to collect fees, not necessarily to make their clients money. For every trade a broker makes, they collect a percentage. This percentage fee is applied whether or not the trade turns out to make money for the investor. So, if an investment management company is handling your 401K, the broker at the company can make deals to invest your money in bonds that will pay them higher fees. Over twenty or thirty years, this can come out to hundreds of thousands of dollars lost on your part, whether the bond investment makes you money or not.

Startled by this lack of transparency and customer service, Peter built his firm around an entirely new model. Creative

Planning would charge a yearly fee between 1 percent and 1.5 percent. That was the only fee they charged, and when it came to the investments they made, they were 100 percent transparent with their investors.

The genius in this strategy is that it aligns Creative Planning's incentives with their customers. At a typical investment management company, brokers are making money through back-door fees. At Creative Planning, their 1 percent to 1.5 percent fee only grows if your portfolio grows, and so that is their sole focus.

In the extremely volatile finance world, it's easy to nickel-and-dime investors who don't know any better. Investment management companies have been doing it for years. Creative Planning, however, took a page out of Amazon's book and put the customer experience first.

The finance world is incredibly uncertain—regulations are constantly changing, and investments are constantly fluctuating in value. In order to truly succeed in that world as an innovator, you need to act proactively and get comfortable with uncertainty. The only standard for your decisions should be, "Is this growing my client's portfolio?"

Digital marketers need to have a similar level of mission focus to succeed in a volatile world.

INTERVIEW: PETER MALLOUK

Peter Mallouk is the CEO of Creative Planning, and has been recognized as one of Worth's Power 100, the world's hundred most powerful men and women in finance. I spoke to him recently about disrupting his industry to take his company to the next level.

I started out as an estate advisor, putting together trusts and wills for clients. I wanted to start my own firm, but I was jaded by the industry, which was not really aligned with the client. Then I thought: *why don't I start a firm and do things differently?*

I wanted to make sure my clients knew the foundational philosophies of investment management, and that they could avoid emotion decisions. When I started my firm, we were different right from the start. We put the client's interests first and created real value that set us apart. We focused on client education and engagement, customizing solutions for clients, and offering planning, legal, and tax solutions as well.

Creative Planning really took off during the financial crisis in 2008. We were like a politician that delivered on a campaign promise; our clients went from fans to advocates. We grew from $100 million in 2004 to $32 billion today, and we're the fastest-growing independent wealth management firm in America.

These days, the industry is changing so quickly that you have to innovate just to stay in the game. It's no longer an option to do it any other way. Otherwise, obsolescence will be at your door fast.

> You don't have to go back to the drawing board and start from scratch; you just have to empower your client. You have to make sure that the actions of your firm are of benefit to your client in the end. You need to be accessible, and you need to think all the way through to the end user to empower them, too.

To see how this works in the political world, political marketers who focus their pitches on their execution rate—voters reached, clicks, donations, data collected—typically have a slight edge. That edge creates more certainty in the mind of the non-political client. I've said for years that corporate media firms know how to paint a beautiful picture, but political media firms know how to target their audience much more effectively.

In addition to execution rates, there are other measurements that translate between the two worlds. For instance, a corporate entity measures its success in profits, while candidates measure success in votes. As consultants, our confidence is grounded in data and the deliverables that stem from it. These deliverables usually come in the form of what we label *actions taken* or *conversions*.

What drives these conversions? Content is a driver, but it's only as good as the audience it was intended for. That means proper targeting is key. The more compatible our creative is to the universe we serve it to, the higher our

LIE #7: IF YOU BRAND
IT, THEY WILL COME

Digital marketing agencies are incentivized to create advertisements around the client's brand *first*, and around the needs or wants of converting the customer second. Their main outcome is to keep their contract as long as possible, and to be paid as much as possible. They push branding first in their ad spend as a mechanism to score a huge advertising budget and bloat their bottom line, instead of doing the on-the-ground work of research and testing to understand what the customer wants and building a strategy around converting customers.

After they've run their large-spend branding campaign, they will propose a conversion campaign. Win-win for the marketing agency—even if it doesn't grow your business.

In politics, on the other hand, we aim to convert voters first and use branding to build loyalty. Political marketers who don't listen to the voters and build their strategy around them are dead in the water. Political marketers *begin* with engagement and conversion, and allow the brand strategy to take shape secondarily. This strategy converts and builds raving fans of the candidate.

Like Creative Planning did, engaging and converting the client first and then creating a flawless experience (branding) is what will build your business more than any digital firm's proposed "brand-first" strategy. You need to demand that your marketing firm helps you convert customers, not just build your brand. It's the whole reason you've hired them—not just to build your brand, but to build your *business*.

conversion rate. Political marketers' ability to marry creative with targeting and speed is what drives action. And a high level of action is what eliminates uncertainty.

MARKETING'S FUTURE IS DEFINED BY UNCERTAINTY

The parallels between the rapid changes in business and marketing are clear. The way we're advertising on behalf of our clients right now will be 1,000 times different in five years.

The people who get in the game right now, that place strategic bets, that act proactively and take calculated risks, are going to come out on top.

Part of the volatility in marketing is that there are a few platforms that really stand out as powerful advertising mediums, and all of them are changing rapidly. For example, we sat in Facebook's offices in 2016, and they told us, "You need to focus on video. Ease off graphic design for your ads, and focus on hiring people who can create great video content."

A year later, this might seem obvious to everyone who has seen Facebook's recent emphasis on video, but at the time, having beautifully designed graphics had been crucial to succeeding on Facebook's platform.

We could have buried our heads in the sand and said, "Well, we're comfortable making graphics, so we're going to continue doing that for now," but we didn't. We're used to the political world, where incredible volatility is just part of the game, and so we changed it up and invested heavily in video, and our business grew.

That was a proactive move, one that required us to embrace uncertainty and leave behind the comfort of our familiar strategies.

Part of the benefit to acting proactively in marketing is that even if you miss the mark, the knowledge you gain will be a huge boon. For example, when Twitter first rose to prominence, famous marketers like Gary Vaynerchuk dedicated themselves to mastering the platform.

Gary in particular is famous for spending hours each day focused on engaging fans via Twitter. Today, Twitter is still a powerful social media platform, but it did not turn out to be the game-changing marketing platform so many people believed it would be.

However, the lessons that marketers like Gary learned

proactively pursuing the platform on Twitter directly translated to later platforms where he had a lot more success. It's no coincidence that many people at the top of their game on other platforms also bet heavily on Twitter.

This is all part of what makes marketing so intimidating to business owners, and what encourages them to keep their heads in the sand and for their digital marketing agencies to take advantage of them. Platforms are always rising and falling, the rules are always changing, and the available technology never stops evolving. When you're busy running a business, you must harness the volatility and turn it to your advantage. Believe me, your competition will be on this road soon; the only question is, who will get there first?

WHO CAN YOU TRUST?

Business owners don't have to be digital marketing experts. What's important is that they work with a trusted marketer to act proactively and adapt when needed.

This doesn't mean you give your marketer full authority to spend infinite money trying every strategy they think of. Remember, "Trust but verify." In this case, that means staying analytical, making your marketer prove their ROI with smaller budgets, but also giving them the leeway to make those calculated bets on the future.

Many businesses want a quick fix. They want to work with a digital marketing company and see quick results, and marketing agencies know this. They'll focus the client on a "brand first" strategy that doesn't have to convert, and run every client through a virtually identical promotion—slap together some creative and pour money into a hot social media platform—before moving onto the next client.

In politics, that would never fly. Politicians who want to get elected have to trust that their marketing team is trying everything they can to win, adapting with the volatility, and leaning into the uncertainty.

As a business owner, you need a digital marketer you can trust on that same level. You need to know that your marketer isn't running a comfortable, one-size-fits-all campaign for you, that they're constantly adapting and iterating, proactively trying to find the strategy that works best for you.

What's great about this is that businesses who are ready to get in the game typically work with marketers who feel the same, and vice versa. For example, after reading this book, if you're a business owner looking to innovate and embrace uncertainty, it's unlikely you'll be impressed with a marketing pitch selling you one type of ad strategy without the research that confirms that assumption, right?

Similarly, as a digital marketer I've turned down multiple political and business clients who were looking for a quick and easy marketing fix. If I can't deliver the long-term result they're looking for with any level of quality, why would I take them on as a client?

Technology has thrown us into a new world when it comes to marketing, and you have the opportunity to be on the cutting edge, the winning side, right now. Yes, it requires letting go of your attachments to the past, and investing in what will work now and in the future—but it's the best money you'll ever spend for your business, and it's the difference between winning and losing the game.

CHALLENGE YOURSELF

1. Name one disruption that will affect your business in the next two years.

2. It sounds easier than it is, but once you get going down the rabbit hole, come up with a few first- and second-order consequences of this disruption.

3. Once you've identified the most likely disruption to impact your business, develop a plan to address it now. Come up with a non-negotiable timeline and a strategy to turn the disruption into a money-making opportunity for your business.

Bonus: What disruption did you identify? How did you handle it, and what lessons can you share with other business owners? I want to hear about it: http://facebook.com/ceophillipstutts.

CONCLUSION

You have nothing to lose and everything to gain from holding your digital marketing firm accountable, or, if called for, firing them now.

But I'll bet you're wondering: do you *really* have to?

This book isn't meant as a one-size-fits-all solution. What I hope you've developed by reading this book is the political mindset that will carry you forward successfully into the new digital marketing future of our changing global economy.

Digital marketers, for all of their innovations and forward advancements, are also living in the past. They're tied to old traditional sales methods for one reason, and one reason alone: these methods are designed to make *them* profit, and not necessarily to make *you* profit. They have little motivation to change their strategies, because right now, they control the game—or, at least, they think they do.

Their mindset is all wrong. Their mindset is not based on winning for you, or getting you to the outcome you want. Their mindset is focused on coming up with a huge budget, using technical jargon to confuse and frighten you into signing a long-term contract, and then running up a huge rate so they can cash your checks.

The mindset that will carry your business into the future is one of innovation and control. You control what happens with your marketing—not your digital marketing firm. That firm works for you, not the other way around. And you can't take a backseat on innovation, because your marketing firm doesn't have the same motivation you do to try new things and innovate for the win. It's up to you to grab the steering wheel and get in the game—cutting a check to a firm of "experts" doesn't relieve you of that responsibility.

Your mindset also has to shift toward building strong, future-proof relationships with your customers. The coming disruption means that, soon, even your most loyal clients or customers *will* have a huge range of other options, and they *will* be tempted to jump ship for something new and shiny. Don't give them a reason to. Your relationships with your clients or customers are what will allow your business not only to survive the tidal wave of change, but to thrive.

What it comes down to is asking your marketing firm the right questions. Dig deep to establish whether they're working for you, or working for themselves. Show them the universal truths laid out in this book, and demand the level of loyalty, service, and success that political marketers provide their clients.

It's up to you to make this happen, and *you can do it*. Don't wait another second—get in the game!

A GIFT FOR YOU!

Still need a little help getting in the game? Well, here's an offer you can't afford to pass up—and I'll only offer it for a limited time.

I've learned through the years that people don't usually go to Home Depot to proactively buy caulk. They go to Home Depot because they need to fill a hole in the wall. It's a reactive purchase.

Much the same manner, most businesses don't want to proactively plan and spend money on marketing, let alone the complicated structure of digital advertising. I wish they understood how important it is to be proactive in their marketing, but too often businesses invest in marketing reluctantly, and in a reactive manner. They ask us to fill the holes. If they see results—a smooth wall—then they'll proactively invest in painting that wall, which leads to sprucing up other parts of the house.

I truly believe marketing firms should be the first ones that invest in the relationships with their clients. Our job is to fill the holes, fix the wall, and hopefully build the client a gorgeous house. That's the commitment we should make, not the other way around.

Want to see how you or your marketing firm is *really* doing? For a limited time, this is your chance to get a risk-free digital marketing audit of your company or non-profit at no cost.

To help you get started, I decided to invest in *your* success by gifting you the same marketing audit my corporate digital marketing agency, Win BIG Media, performs for our top clients (at a cost of $5,000). We'll audit your website, social media presence and platforms, and budget. We'll score all of it, and identify the holes, what you can improve, and how much your business or marketing agency has wasted. And if they *have* wasted your money, this audit will be the ammunition you need to fire them now.

On the flip side, if your marketing firm is doing a great job, we'll tell you that, too. You really don't have anything to lose, and you have no obligation to hire my firm; this audit is a gift to you.

Take the final challenge today!

You can email me for the audit at PS@phillipstutts.com, or go to http://phillipstutts.com/audit to get started!

ABOUT PHILLIP STUTTS'S COMPANIES

Win BIG Media, Phillip Stutts & Company, and Go BIG Media, Inc. are a consortium of three outcome-driven companies launched by Phillip Stutts. The ethos for each company is service and growth, and each accomplishes this for its clients day in and day out.

Win BIG Media is a corporate marketing agency that leverages the latest in business and political strategy, technology, and design to tell stories, disrupt markets, and win the day for corporate clients—every day. You can reach the team at Win BIG Media here: winbigmedia.com

Go BIG Media Inc., a political media and marketing firm, that has received national acclaim for its work on behalf of U.S. Senators, Governors, and presidential candidates. Notably, it has won over 20 awards for its excellence in political advertising, including a "Pollie" award from the American Association of Political Consultants for "Best Digital/Internet Independent Expenditure Presidential Campaign" and a Peer Choice Award for "Digital Video Excellence in a Presidential Campaign." You can reach the team at Go BIG here: gobigmediainc.com

Phillip Stutts & Company is an exclusive private consulting practice, where Phillip personally works with elite CEOs and non-profit leaders to bring their business and marketing to the next level. You can book Phillip to speak, subscribe to his special offers, and sign up for regular updates on his take on the marketing world through his website PhillipStutts.com.

THE STORY BEHIND THE ETHOS

In 2011, Phillip Stutts saw the political and corporate winds changing to an all-digital advertising world. He dug in and spent the next few years researching and meeting with more than 100 CEOs, corporate marketing agencies, and political digital media firms across the country.

He found most marketing firms to be smart, creative, and

likable. But he found two *huge* mistakes they all made consistently: they struggled to put their clients' outcomes first, and they failed to provide great customer service.

Each CEO he interviewed was frustrated or had fired their marketing agency. On the political side, each digital marketing firm he talked with complained that their political candidates and their campaigns were the problem, and that it was hard work to make clients happy.

The industry was missing a competitor whose dedication to ethics, honesty and client satisfaction emanated throughout. Seeing the gap in the marketplace, Phillip created Go BIG Media and Win BIG Media on an ethos of service, transparency, and excellence, with a mission to totally disrupt the industry. Both agencies were founded upon a culture of service (they even have a Director of Culture—who kicks ass!).

Go BIG and Win BIG's core values of growth and service to others before self are non-negotiable and drive everything the company does, from hiring to client results and personal development.

The result? Since launching, Phillip's companies have exceeded 500% year over year growth and donated over $100,000 to charity, and his employees have volunteered over 1,000 hours to their local communities. And they are just getting started.

ABOUT THE AUTHOR

PHILLIP STUTTS has more than twenty years of political and business marketing experience. He has contributed to more than one thousand election victories of senators, governors, representatives, and two US presidents. In 2015, Phillip founded his political and corporate digital marketing firm helping politicians, small businesses, and multiple Fortune 200 companies. His agency has already won more than twenty prestigious honors, including the award for Digital Video Excellence in a Presidential Campaign. Phillip is a regular guest on CNN, Fox News, and MSNBC, making more than two hundred appearances in the past five years, and has been referred to as "a political guru" by ESPN and a "marketing genius" on Fox Business. Follow Phillip on Facebook at /ceophillipstutts or on Twitter @phillipstutts.

CPSIA information can be obtained
at www.ICGtesting.com
Printed in the USA
BVHW01*0158200118
505807BV00004B/7/P